A NATION
OF NEWCOMERS

A NATION OF NEWCOMERS

ETHNIC MINORITIES IN AMERICAN HISTORY

BY J. JOSEPH HUTHMACHER

DELACORTE PRESS / NEW YORK

Published by
Dell Publishing Co., Inc.
750 Third Avenue
New York, New York 10017
Library of Congress Catalog Card Number: 68-1100
Manufactured in the United States of America
Second Printing November 1970

 CONTENTS

A NATION
OF NEWCOMERS

I. INTRODUCTION: A NATION OF IMMIGRANTS

BY THE TIME the thirteen American colonies were ready to fight for independence and establish a new nation, their free population (excluding about 400,000 Negro slaves) already consisted of a mixture of people descended from a wide variety of European backgrounds and ethnic stocks. Of the approximately 1,850,000 people living in the colonies in 1765, the best estimates are that 65 to 70 per cent of them were English, while another 15 to 20 per cent came from the other parts of Great Britain—Scotland, Wales, and Ireland. But there were also about 175,000 Germans, 55,000 Hollanders, 40,000 Frenchmen, 20,000 Swiss, 15,000 Swedes, and perhaps 1,500 Jews. "Here individuals of all nations are melted into a new race of men," wrote St. John de Crèvecoeur, a colonist from France who considered himself an American even before the Revolution. "*He* is an American," Crèvecoeur continued, "who, leaving behind him all his ancient prejudices and manners, receives new ones from the new mode of life he has embraced. . . ."

Crèvecoeur's prediction that the New World would produce "one of the finest systems of population which has ever appeared"—who "will one day cause great changes in the world"—has certainly come true. Nevertheless, the "melting" process which he described—and later Americans often described their nation as a "melting pot"—never did operate with the complete thoroughness that he imagined. For neither before Crèvecoeur's time nor after did the immigrant groups who came from abroad leave behind *all* of their "ancient prejudices and manners." The Scotch, Welsh, Irish, Germans, Dutch, French, Swiss, Swedes, and Jews who came to America before 1776 each brought with them languages, religions, customs, arts, foods, and notions of politics and philosophy particular to their homelands. So did the settlers from England, and because they came earliest and in the largest numbers, English ways of doing things left the biggest mark of all on the American way of life as it gradually took form. The successive waves of immigrants that came after the Revolution, from still other lands, would bring their own cultures with them, too.

Because of the diverse origins of the people who settled here, ethnic minorities and minority problems inevitably arose in America. A minority exists whenever a group senses that its distinctive characteristics separate its members from the dominant group in society in ways that impose handicaps upon them. The problems arise when the minority group's aspirations to win acceptance, and equality of opportunity, clash with the dominant group's natural desire to preserve its favored position. It is important to remember that the minority need not always be *numerically* smaller than the dominant group. Possession of social, econom-

ic, and political *power* in the society concerned is
the real secret of the dominant group's success. Moreover, members of a group which is considered a minority at one time, or in one part of the country, might
not find themselves so considered at a later time, or in
another locality.

In short, the identification of a minority group is a
relative matter—relative to time, place, and circum-
stance. But because America is such a large country,
and one which has been settled by peoples of many
different origins and backgrounds, she has always
had minorities and minority problems.

Examples of the conflict between ethnic minorities
and dominant groups abound during colonial times,
and frequently the result was injustice and persecution. The Quakers, who long dominated Pennsylvania
politics, for example, frequently seemed intent on
denying the German minority in the western part of
the colony their full rights. At the same time, however,
Quakers were very unpopular in Puritan New England; indeed, several of them had been put to death in
Massachusetts for holding firm to their religious beliefs. Catholics, Jews, and other religious minorities
suffered discrimination in almost all the colonies. Up
and down the coastal seaboard, differences between
various nationality groups early produced hard feeling,
name-calling, and sometimes even violence.

Nonetheless, it is generally true that by the end of
the colonial period diverse ethnic groups lived in
greater harmony in America than in most parts of Europe at the time. Just because there were so *many*
different kinds of people in America, the various na-

tionality and religious groups had begun to learn that
if they expected to win toleration for themselves, they
must show a greater toleration for others. Moreover,
many colonists had begun to sense that each of the
different groups among them was capable of making
valuable contributions out of its cultural luggage, to
the advancement of the common welfare. Intermarriage among persons of different nationalities and religions fostered mutual understanding and made people
more elastic in their practices and beliefs. Finally, the
abundance of land and of opportunity for work in
America, combined with the shortage of labor, took
some of the edge off the economic competition which
frequently deepens the ethnic divisions within a population. In America, a Land of Plenty, there seemed to
be room and need for muscles and brains from all
countries.

So it was that in declaring their independence in
1776 the leaders of the Revolution, most of whom belonged to the predominant English and Protestant
majority of the population, nonetheless proclaimed
that "*all* men are created equal . . . endowed by their
Creator with certain unalienable Rights." Among the
charges listed against King George III in the Declaration of Independence was the complaint that he had
attempted to restrict the immigration of non-English
persons to America. Of the fifty-six signers of the Declaration, a considerable number were colonists who
were not of English birth or descent.

Xenophobia (suspicion and dislike of foreigners)
and ethnocentrism (the tendency to boast about what
are considered the superior characteristics of one's

own ethnic group) had by no means disappeared by
the time the United States began her career as an in-
dependent nation. Indeed as early as 1798, in the Alien
and Sedition Acts, the Federalist Party sought to limit
the political power of recent immigrants, who supposedly were voting for the Federalists' opponents.
But most "native" Americans at this time undoubtedly
shared the sentiments of their first President, George
Washington, who on Thanksgiving Day 1795 urged
his countrymen "humbly and fervently to beseech the
kind Author of these blessings . . . to render this
country more and more a safe and propitious asylum
for the unfortunate of other countries." When the
Alien and Sedition laws were allowed to expire in
1801, President Thomas Jefferson expressed the pre-
vailing sentiment of Americans when he asked: "Shall
we refuse to the unhappy fugitives from distress that
hospitality which the savages of the wilderness extended to our fathers arriving in this land? Shall oppressed humanity find no asylum on this globe?"

The views of Washington and Jefferson underlay
the liberal immigration policy followed by the United
States through most of the nineteenth century. Beginning in the 1880s the doors to America were partially
shut—first to immigrants from the Orient, and then, in
the 1920s, to people from abroad in general. But in the
meantime some forty millions of foreigners came to
this nation's shores in search of political and religious
freedom and economic betterment. They contributed
their brawn and brains to the remarkable economic
development of the American continent that took
place in these years, and each of the many ethnic

groups among them contributed out of its particular culture to the enrichment of America's own culture.

But the presence of these successive waves of newcomers severely tested the tolerant principles proclaimed by the older settlers in the Declaration of Independence and other documents which they revered. Each of the immigrant minority groups learned what it meant to suffer some degree of ridicule, abuse, and discrimination. Yet with experience, education, and sufficient time to prove its worth, each of these minorities made progress toward winning acceptance, first for individual members from within its ranks and then, gradually, for the group as a whole.

Moreover, as the minorities struggled to maintain that equality of opportunity which was essential to their own advancement, they served also constantly to remind the older settlers of the value of the ideals of freedom proclaimed by the nation's Founding Fathers. As the late President John F. Kennedy wrote, the immigrant minorities "infused the nation with a commitment to far horizons and new frontiers, and thereby kept the pioneer spirit of American life, the spirit of equality and hope, always alive and strong."

The integration of many ethnic minorities and their cultures into the mainstream of American life, which is in large part the story of America, is in the end a success story. But is has been also, at times, a sad story, marked by heartbreak and frustration. In this book we shall examine in some detail the experience—sad and happy—of a few of the minority groups of the nineteenth and twentieth centuries. It should be remembered that these groups are representative only—

representative of many other minority groups from which a large part of today's American population is descended.

Hopefully, too, we may learn some helpful lessons from this survey of the treatment that has been accorded ethnic minority groups in our democratic society. For, despite the ending of large-scale immigration in the 1920s, we Americans—who have inherited a big country—still have many minorities among us. By reviewing our past, Americans of the present generation may succeed in avoiding some of the mistakes made by earlier generations—mistakes that account for many of the darker, unhappier pages of our national record.

II. THE OLD IMMIGRATION: THE CATHOLIC IRISH

UNTIL THE 1880s most immigrants to the United States continued to come from the countries of northern and western Europe. Since the American Revolution nearly five million more settlers have come from England, Scotland, Wales, and Northern Ireland. They quickly blended into and reinforced the British, Protestant majority who had become the predominant element of America's population during the colonial period.

From Germany have come nearly seven million additional immigrants, while the Scandinavian countries —Sweden, Norway, Denmark, and Finland—sent about two and one half million. Adjustment to America, and to the people already here, was harder for these non-British peoples. English was not their mother tongue. Although most of them were Protestants, their forms of Protestantism differed from those practiced by most of the English-speaking Americans. Some of the more puritanical of the native Yankees frowned, for example, when German immigrants picnicked, played ball, and even drank beer on Sunday after attending church services; there were even riots at times when the "natives" sought to prevent these immigrants from indulging in their traditional "Continental Sunday" pastimes. Because their language and customs made them seem different, German and Scandinavian immigrants were taunted frequently with nicknames—such as "Krauts" and "Norskis." Sometimes they suffered even harsher forms of discrimination in the communities where they settled.

But America was still a basically agricultural nation, blessed with abundant land, during the early and mid-nineteenth century when the bulk of these Old Immigrant peoples arrived. As a result, a great many of them were able to acquire farms and, after a time, to blend in with the rest of America's agricultural population. By the beginning of the twentieth century they and their descendants populated much of the country's midwestern states. Their differences were no longer so visible or so disturbing and, generally speaking, they had come to be considered part of the dominant "native" element of Americans.

The *most* different of all the nineteenth-century Old Immigrant groups, however, were the Catholic Irish, who came from the southern counties of the Emerald Isle. A relatively small number, fleeing years of religious and political persecution under British rule at home, had migrated to America before 1776. Their love of liberty and hatred of despotism made them ardent patriots at the time of the American Revolution. But it was not until after the War of 1812, when economic conditions worsened in Ireland, that Catholic Irish peasants began arriving in the United States in large numbers. In the century after 1820 some four and a quarter million immigrants came from Ireland. A great many of them made the move when, in the 1840s, a series of potato-crop failures produced famine at home. As one writer described conditions in Ireland at the time: "The smell of the potato rotting in the fields rose and mingled with the odors of death in the cottages and along the hedgerows." Under such conditions of misery, it seemed that whole villages uprooted themselves and migrated to the New World.

The conditions of the voyage to America, especially before the introduction of steamships in the 1860s, almost defy description. The vessels were small, and hundreds of immigrants were packed into their cramped holds without adequate light, ventilation, or sanitation facilities. Sometimes the food and water—which immigrants were expected to provide for themselves—ran out, and then they would be at the mercy of extortionate ship captains. Cholera and other diseases frequently ravaged the steerage passengers. Sometimes half, or more, of a ship's human cargo never lived to see the New World. In 1847 alone, more than ten thousand Irish immigrants died while en route to America.

The Irish who survived and reached the Land of Promise, however, soon found that their difficulties had only begun. Like the Germans and Scandinavians, they were, of course, a minority group, and their foreignness to the ways of American natives seemed even more pronounced. For one thing, these southern Irishmen were Catholics, in contrast to most of the natives and the other Old Immigrant groups. It should be remembered, too, that many of them at first spoke only Gaelic and knew no English. In addition, the men and women from the south of Ireland shared a hatred of England that knew no bounds, while England was the mother country of many Americans. Finally, of all the Old Immigrant groups, the Irish on the whole were the most poverty-stricken upon their arrival in this country. Penniless and stranded, most of them found it impossible to purchase farms and thus disperse themselves across the countryside. Instead, they congregated in the cities. As a result, "natives" were made more aware of their presence and of their difference than might otherwise have been the case. The Catholic Irish were the most visible of all the Old Immigrants; consequently, it took them longer than the others to achieve adjustment and win acceptance.

Hard feeling against the Irish—the "Paddies" or "Micks"—sometimes erupted into outright violence. In Boston in 1834 and in Philadelphia in 1844, for example, mobs burned convents housing groups of immigrant nuns.

When it came to the vital matter of finding jobs, the Irish-Americans found themselves discriminated against by native employers and workers alike. Signs reading "No Irish Need Apply" were a common sight. Moreover, they were further handicapped by their lack of skills, for most of them had been peasant farmers in the old country. They seemed to be eligible for only the meaner sorts of jobs: as dock workers, ditch diggers, and manual laborers. Many of them joined canal and railroad construction gangs—fortunately there was much building to be done in nineteenth-century

America—at wages that averaged a dollar a day. Some of them went to work in coal mines—at eighty-five cents a day. Gradually the Irish began displacing the older immigrant groups as unskilled machine operators in the textile mills and other factories that spread out from New England as American industry grew. But the father's and sons' wages often were still not enough to support the family; then the mother and daughters took in laundry, or got jobs as domestic servants in the homes of the wealthy who owned the docks, the construction companies, and the factories.

Life was hard for these early Irish settlers, and that fact was reflected in the high rates of disease, mental illness, and alcoholism that prevailed among them. Some sought the easy way out, and turned to gambling, racketeering, criminal gangs, and other forms of delinquent behavior. The vast majority of hardier souls, however, worked, saved, and persevered, and took consolation from the institutions and organizations that they developed in the midst of their often hostile environment. They had their own neighborhoods—even though usually they were only "shanty towns" on "the wrong side of the tracks"—where they could at least find human warmth and understanding among people of their own kind. There were organizations like the Friendly Sons of Saint Patrick, the Hibernians, and the Charitable Irish Societies which provided assistance to the swarms of new immigrants still arriving.

In addition, many cities soon had theaters that specialized in presenting plays and music which reminded the Irishmen of their native country. There were Irish-American newspapers, which kept readers informed of events in their homeland and at the same time served to familiarize them with the affairs of their new country. There were individuals who achieved success in America and in whom the Irish-American masses could take pride. Often success was most easily attained in athletics, where a man's religion and nationality did not count so heavily against him. Fighters like Paddy Ryan, John L. Sullivan, Jake Kilrain, and James Corbett—whose feats in the prize ring won the admiration of all Americans—provided the Irish-Americans with some of their earliest folk heroes.

Above all there was the Catholic Church, which assured the immigrants that their daily struggles and sufferings did have meaning after all—meaning that would be revealed in the rewards of eternal salvation. The priesthood afforded another avenue whereby young Irish-Americans might rise to positions that commanded respect. Many of them chose that vocation, which is the reason why the Irish have long been so prominent in the American Catholic Church and its hierarchy. To build their parishes and to support the priests who brought so much consolation into their often dreary lives, Irish-Americans made great financial sacrifices. It all seemed worthwhile to them, however, for their religion was in some ways their main source of self-help.

The Irish also adopted other, more worldly, means of self-help in their attempts to better the conditions of their lives. Labor organizations were one of the most effective methods. At first, in response to the repressive measures that employers used against them, such groups sometimes resorted to radical methods. The Molly Maguires, a secret society organized among Irish-American coal miners in western Pennsylvania in the 1850s, were guilty of arson, blackmail, and violence in their attempts to win concessions from the mine owners. The more responsible leaders of the miners, together with the Catholic clergy, denounced the Mollies, and after some of its members were hanged for murder in 1875, the organization disbanded.

As public acceptance of labor's right to organize advanced, however, Irish-Americans remained prominent in the more orderly labor movements that resulted. They played a large part in the Knights of Labor, who enjoyed some success in the 1880s under the leadership of an Irishman named Terence Powderley. Another famous Catholic Irish labor leader, John Mitchell, pioneered in the formation of the United Mine Workers of America in the 1890s. And it was perhaps symbolic that when the American Federation of Labor and the Congress of Industrial Organizations merged in 1955, the first president of the united movement was George Meany, a labor spokesman of Catholic Irish descent.

Political activity was another means whereby the Irish immigrants sought to improve their lot. In Ireland they had been the victims of political oppression, but in America they had the right to vote once they were naturalized, and they seemed eager to participate in the government of their new country.

As the number of Irish-American voters grew, particularly in the cities of the northeastern part of the country, politicians began to compete for their support. Since the natives who looked down upon the immigrants seemed to prefer the Whig and then the Republican parties, the Irish-Americans were more inclined to become Democrats. Political bosses arose in many cities who helped the newcomers secure jobs—frequently on the city's payroll—and who provided the poverty-stricken immigrants with aid when emergencies such as sickness, death, or unemployment arose. Often the boss's headquarters in each ward—perhaps a store or a saloon—served also as a social center for the immigrant neighborhood. Usually he sponsored picnics, balls, and other activities which brought some merriment into their grim lives. In return for all this, the newcomers voted for the boss's candidates.

Unfortunately, the boss often indulged in corruption and graft, too. Through his control of City Hall, he sold construction contracts and other privileges to unscrupulous businessmen willing to pay his price; sometimes he sold protection to criminals and racketeers. It was from these sources that the boss secured the money to provide assistance to the immigrant voters—and to pad his own pockets as well.

Native Americans interested in reforming politics constantly denounced the boss and his machine, and often they attacked the immigrants for supporting him in return for the assistance he gave them. At times nativist political movements sought to limit the political rights of the Catholic Irish and other immigrant groups: the Know-Nothing Party of the 1850s and the American Protective Association of the 1890s are examples. In defense of the minority groups it might be

pointed out that, for a long time, few others except the
machine politicians seemed to show any interest in
helping them when emergencies arose. Hardly any
public agencies existed to which they might turn in
times of crisis. Was it not natural, then, that they
should support the boss who seemed to be conscious
of their needs?

Eventually, after the beginning of the twentieth
century, Americans became more aware of the desir-
ability of having the government provide greater security for the immigrant working class, at public expense. During the so-called Progressive Era
(1900–1917) laws were adopted which provided better regulation of working conditions in factories and
living conditions in tenements, free public employment
agencies, workmen's compensation insurance, public
playgrounds, better educational facilities, and the like.
Later, during the New Deal and after, these reforms
were extended to include such things as unemployment insurance, old-age pensions, Medicare, public
housing, and urban renewal projects.

In promoting such liberal measures native American
reformers were joined by a more mature, broader-vi-
sioned generation of politicians who sprang from the
ranks of the immigrant masses themselves. One of
them was David Ignatius Walsh, who became the first
Catholic Irish Governor of Massachusetts in 1913 and
who demonstrated a keen interest in labor and educational reforms during his administration. Another was
Charles F. Murphy, an Irish Catholic who as the head
of New York City's Tammany Hall from 1902 until
1924 displayed unusual sympathy (for a boss) with

many social welfare reform proposals. One of Murphy's protégés, Alfred E. Smith, was the reform-minded Democratic leader in the New York state legislature during the Progressive Era. As Governor of New York during the 1920s, Smith provided a model progressive administration for his state. In 1928, when the Democratic Party nominated him for President, Smith became the first Irish Catholic to seek the highest office in the land.

Irish Catholic politicians thus played an important part in the early development of modern American liberalism. During the New Deal and since then many of them have continued to be prominent in the ranks of liberal political movements. Consequently they have helped foster greater security, and equality of opportunity, not only for themselves but for all minority groups and for Americans in general. They helped develop our present-day system of liberal capitalism in which most Americans take pride and which we hope may be a model for people elsewhere in the world.

Another reliance on which the early Catholic Irish immigrants staked their hopes for advancement was education. The ditch diggers, miners, machine tenders, and servant girls of the first generations were determined that their sons and daughters should know a better way of life. To that end they strove to keep their children in schools—preferably ones where the doctrines of their Catholic faith, as well as more worldly knowledge, might be learned. Their hard-won earnings went into the building of parochial schools and to the support of Catholic institutions of higher learning such as Holy Cross College, Fordham, Villanova, Notre

Dame, St. Louis University, the Catholic University of America, and Georgetown.

From such schools—and from the public schools and universities as well—there flowed each year a swelling wave of Catholic Irishmen fully equipped to fill better positions than their parents: in skilled crafts, in supervisory and clerical jobs, in business and finance, in the professions, sciences, and the arts. Slowly, as individuals proved their worth in those pursuits and occupations, doors that had been closed by discrimination began to open wider to members of the Catholic Irish minority. And as native Americans allowed themselves to rub elbows more often with Irish-Americans—on the job, in better neighborhoods, and socially—their previous prejudices began to melt away. Maybe those "Micks" weren't such a bad lot after all!

By the time Al Smith was nominated for President in 1928, politics, sports, and the religious life had long ceased to limit the ambitions of the Irish-American minority. Its members had distinguished themselves in every imaginable field. Thomas Fortune Ryan, Cornelius F. Kelly, and James A. Farrell were just a few of the Irishmen whose names stood at the top of American business's "Who's Who." Frank Walsh, Bourke Cockran, and Frank Murphy were nationally recognized lawyers. Michael M. O'Shaughnessy had made engineering history with his bridges and tunnels. Individuals like John Boyle O'Reilly and Joyce Kilmer and the brilliant tenor John McCormack had left indelible marks in the realms of literature and music. The great mass of Irish-Americans who continued to work at more ordinary occupations were now, more often than not, to be found among the foremen and supervisors and in white-collar jobs.

And on a typical evening in Al Smith's beloved New York City it would not be unusual to find an Irish-American coed of Hunter College (named after Thomas Hunter, an Irish Catholic educator who championed higher education for women) riding a subway (built by Nicholas Brady) to Grand Central Station (planned by John F. O'Rourke), shopping in a chain store (an idea originated by James Butler) and then making her way to a Broadway theater (possibly owned by Joseph P. Kennedy) to enjoy a popular musical of the day (probably written by George M. Cohan).

Yet Al Smith lost the election of 1928, and some aspects of his defeat indicated that prejudice against the Catholic Irish was still strong in many parts of the country. Not until thirty-two years later—when John F. Kennedy was elected president in 1960—could the Catholic Irish feel certain that all of America's rewards, even the highest office in the land, were open to them on a basis of full equality with "native" Americans. When Kennedy was elected, according to some writers, the Irish-Americans' position as a minority group in the United States officially ended. But remember that it had taken more than a hundred years to bring full-fledged acceptance about!

Today the Irish frequently are not even mentioned in books dealing with American minority groups. Perhaps, on St. Patrick's Day, Irish-Americans assembled in banquet halls do recall the trials and tribulations of the immigrants from whom they are descended. But the program for the affair will feature typical American figures known and respected throughout the land. The master of ceremonies might well be a leading television or motion-picture personality: Ed Sullivan, for example, or Bing Crosby. After the guests had consumed their typically American meal of corned beef and cabbage, songs now as familiar in America as they once were in Ireland might be sung by Dennis Day, or Metropolitan Opera star Brian Sullivan. All-American athletes, whose distinctively Irish names have become familiar in every household, might then be introduced. Next the audience would be addressed by a prominent member of Congress—Senate Majority Leader Mike Mansfield or Speaker of the House John W. McCormack, for example—or by an eminent jurist such as Supreme Court Justice William J. Brennan. When the festivities were finished, applause would ring out not only from the Irish-American descendants present but from the many "native" citizens who had been invited. For St. Patrick's Day is now an "All American" holiday.

On the whole, then, in recent years Irish-Americans have become accepted as part of the predominant majority of the American population. As that process has taken place, however, some members of this former minority have shown a regrettable tendency to display, toward other minority groups, the same types of intolerance and discrimination once practiced against their own forbears. Forgetful of their own past, they are forgetful of the times when, as in the 1860s, American newspapers described the Catholic Irish immigrant as one who

> never knew an hour of civilized society . . . born savage—as brutal a ruffian as an untamed Indian. . . . The born criminal and pauper . . . a pitiful spectacle of a man . . . pushed straight to hell by that abomination against common sense called the Catholic religion. . . . To compare him with an intelligent [Negro] would be an insult to the latter. . . . Scratch a convict or a pauper, and the chances are that you tickle the skin of an Irish Catholic.

It is well, then, that today's Irish-Americans, and all Americans, should remember—more frequently than on St. Patrick's Day—the handicaps under which the first waves of Catholic Irish immigrants to this country labored. We should recall, too, the long and arduous journey which they and their descendants have had to make in order to enjoy full rights and equality of opportunity in this Land of Promise. For as President Kennedy has written of his own ancestors and of all other immigrant groups: "We must know how they met the new land and how it met them, and, most important, we must know what these things mean for our present and for our future."

III. THE NEW IMMIGRATION: THE ITALIANS

BY THE LATE NINETEENTH CENTURY many members of the Old Immigrant minorities from northern and western Europe—including even the Catholic Irish—had begun to improve their economic and social position in America. Now, their places at the bottom rungs of society were being filled in turn by vast new waves of immigrants pouring into the United States from other parts of Europe. As Irishmen moved up to better positions, for example, their former jobs, on the wharves, in the mines, and in railroad and construction gangs were taken over by immigrants from Italy, the Balkan countries, Greece, and other areas of southern Europe. As Irishmen increasingly became able to move out of the worst slums to better neighborhoods, the tenements they left behind might be occupied by Jews, Poles, Slavs, Russians, and other newcomers arriving from eastern Europe.

In the 1880s immigrants from these new sources began to outweigh the number coming to America from the older sources in northwestern Europe. Although people from the Old Immigration countries continued to arrive during the following decades, their number

was soon overwhelmed by the newer stocks. Since 1880
the countries of southern and eastern Europe have
provided America with about fifteen million settlers.

Not just the number of these New Immigrants, as
they came to be called, was impressive. In the eyes of
"native" Americans these hordes of newcomers seemed
to be even stranger and more different than the Old
Immigrants had appeared to be earlier. For one thing,
their languages were even more foreign to the basically English, or American, tongue. In appearance they
were frequently of darker complexion; also their native costumes and customs seemed more outlandish.
Few of them were Protestants; even among the many
who were Catholics, the saints most honored and the
feasts most carefully observed differed from those of
the Catholic Irish. Educational facilities were less
available in the countries from which the New Immigrants came than in northwestern Europe; hence a
larger proportion of them were illiterate when they got
here. The levels of skill acquired in industry and farming were usually lower in their homelands, too. And,
generally speaking, they arrived in the United States
with even less money in their pockets than had the
earlier immigrant groups—with the possible exception
of the Irish.

On top of all this, the New Immigrants were coming
into a country which was itself undergoing a great
transformation. By the late nineteenth century land
for farming was becoming scarcer and therefore cost-
lier. Moreover, relatively fewer hands were needed
now to produce America's crops as farm technology
made tremendous advances. More and more the na-

tion's economic life was centering on manufacturing and commercial business, carried on in cities.

In short, in the late nineteenth century the United States felt the full impact of the Industrial Revolution. What had formerly been an essentially agricultural, rural nation was being transformed rapidly into an essentially industrial, urban civilization. Thus, more so than in the past, opportunities for immigrants to make a living seemed to be limited to the cities. More than the earlier groups of newcomers, therefore—again with the possible exception of the Irish—the New Immigrants congregated in the cities. And as in the case of the Irish, this tendency made their difference from other Americans stand out. In a rapidly changing and troubled America, the New Immigrants were extremely visible.

Indeed, according to many historians, the changes taking place in the American environment—and *not* the supposedly greater foreignness of the New Immigrants' ways—were the main cause of the seemingly greater difficulties of adjustment which they encountered, compared with some Old Immigrant groups. Unfortunately, however, many "native" Americans failed for a long time to appreciate this fact. Instead, the natives emphasized the cultural differences between the Old and New Immigrants and tended toward the conclusion that the ways of the New Immigrants could not be assimilated to "American" ways. Gradually their hostility to the newer-comers grew until, in the 1920s, it produced important changes in America's immigration policies and in the nation's general attitude toward its minorities as well.

Largest of all the New Immigrant groups were the Italians. The discoverer of the New World had been an Italian, of course, and America got its name from another Italian explorer, Amerigo Vespucci. An Italian political philosopher who migrated to Virginia, Filippo Mazzei, became a close friend of Thomas Jefferson and other Revolutionary leaders; it is believed that some of the very phrases used in the Declaration of Independence are attributable to his influence. During the first half of the nineteenth century other political refugees from Italy came to our shores. So did a number of entertainers, musicians, and artists. One Italian, Filippo Traetta, founded the American Conservatory of Music in 1800; another, Lorenzo da Ponte, brought the first opera company to New York in 1832. Constantino Brumidi, "the Michelangelo of the Capitol," painted the impressive historical scenes that adorn the rotunda of our Capitol building in Washington.

Yet in 1850 there were only four thousand Italian-born people living in America. It was not until the 1880s that masses of poorer,. unskilled Italian peasants began arriving here in large numbers. Since the beginning of that movement, about five million have come.

In the case of these immigrants, political or religious persecution played little part as motives for leaving their homeland. Rather it was the abject poverty of their existence that made them depart. In southern Italy, where most of them came from, a semifeudal land system still prevailed in the late nineteenth century. Most of the land was owned by aristocrats; peasant families were forced to divide and subdivide their little plots among their children until virtually no opportunity remained for an individual to make ends meet. As a few pioneer immigrants to America sent back word about the jobs available in the New World, more and more Italians decided to seek improvement in the land of opportunity.

Many Italians came to the United States with the hope that here they might save enough money to purchase larger farms for themselves in Italy. A considerable proportion of them did return to their "old country" in the years between 1880 and 1920—"birds of passage" they were called. Some "native" Americans resented this tendency among the Italian and other New Immigrant groups. They came here "only to get rich at our expense," some charged—forgetting that while the immigrants were here, they helped to develop and enrich America's growing economy, too.

But this factor, added to all of the cultural differences that marked the Italians and New Immigrants, helped account for the unhospitable reception which they frequently encountered in America. From time to time anti-Italian riots commanded national headlines, as "native" workers in various cities and mill towns protested that immigrants willing to work for low wages were stealing their jobs. Hostility, resentment, and discrimination were the common lot of the "Dagoes and Wops," whether they were "birds of passage" or not.

Of the many Italian immigrants who became permanent residents of the United States, fewer than 10 per cent entered agricultural pursuits, despite the fact that more than three-fourths of them had been peasant farmers formerly. Colonies of Italian settlers did establish vineyards in California and in the Finger Lakes region of New York, laying the basis for the wine industries which flourish in those states today. Other Italians developed successful truck farms in the outlying districts of large cities and grew the fresh fruit and vegetables transported daily to the tables of nearby city dwellers. Some went to work on cotton and cane sugar plantations in the South; Italians also became prominent in the fishing industries of the Gulf of Mexico and Pacific Coast states.

But the overwhelming majority of Italians remained in the cities, where jobs for their unskilled hands seemed to be most readily available. In securing work on the docks, on construction projects, or with railroad gangs, the Italian immigrant frequently relied upon the neighborhood *padrone* (or "work boss"). The *padrone* was one of the immigrants' own countrymen, but usually one who had been in America longer and who had developed contacts with employers of unskilled labor. To fill their needs he recruited work gangs of newly arrived immigrants settling in his bailiwick—collecting a fee from both the employer and the job-seekers in return for his service. Frequently the *padrone* also served as his neighborhood's banker, loan office, travel agent, interpreter, and legal counselor, providing an intermediary in the immigrants' dealings with the police and other officials of the strange outside world. All too often, unfortunately, unscrupulous *padrones* took unfair advantage of their countrymen. Moreover, "native" Americans viewed the immigrants' dependence on the *padrone* system as an indication that they lacked initiative and self-reliance. In the general absence of public, tax-supported agencies to serve their needs, however, the immigrants for a long time had no other alternative but to pay the *padrone's* price.

In other instances peace-loving Italian immigrants were preyed upon by secret, terroristic organizations. In Italy societies like the Mafia had originated to enforce justice where the local police and the ruling aristocracy failed to do so; American pioneers had formed somewhat similar vigilante groups in frontier areas. When transported to America, however, the Mafia and other societies came under the control of criminal elements. They indulged in racketeering, blackmail, and extortion, and they did not stop at employing physical violence and even murder against their victims. Responsible Italian-Americans condemned such organizations but—as in the case of the Molly Maguires among the Irish—their activities tended to cast an unfavorable light on the Italian-American population as a whole.

In response to the internal dangers and external hostility which they faced in their new environment, Italian-Americans at first sought self-protection by drawing within themselves in a way that was similar to the reaction of the Irish and other minority groups. Individuals settled in neighborhoods where their countrymen already were—and thus "little Italys" developed in most of America's large cities. Indeed since Italy was a very provincial country until well into the twentieth century, immigrants even sought out earlier arrivals who had lived in the very same town in Italy. Some tenement houses in New York City came to be inhabited almost entirely by immigrants from the same Italian village.

Soon the Italian-Americans also had their own immigrant-aid and fraternal societies, which frequently provided sickness and death insurance benefits for their members. The Sons of Italy, organized early in this century, brought many of these local lodges together into a national federation. Some societies emphasized the preservation of Italian music and other aspects of the homeland's culture. Italian-American newspapers served the same purposes as Irish-American journals. The largest of them, *Il Progresso Italo-Americano*, was founded in 1880, and soon many others were being published in major cities.

The Catholic faith was, of course, one of the most important parts of the culture which most Italian immigrants brought with them. But the earlier arrivals often felt uneasy worshipping in the existing churches, most of which were staffed by Irish priests who knew neither the language nor the religious customs of the Italian people. With much effort and sacrifice Italian-Americans in many areas gradually built churches, served by priests of their own stock, where the particularly Italian aspects of their Catholicism might be preserved. In many Italian-American neighborhoods traditional feasts were observed, where devotion to a patron saint was mingled with colorful street parades, entertainment, and a general holiday atmosphere.

In Italy, more so than in many other countries, the family was a closely knit unit. In each household the father's word carried undoubted authority, while the mother was expected to provide the warmth and affec-

tion that would add to the ties of devotion. The children were to be respectful and obedient, while their
parents schooled them for their future obligations as
adults. In its wider scope too the family, embracing
grandparents, aunts, uncles, cousins, and godparents,
possessed an unusual degree of solidarity in Italy. Indeed, faithfulness to one's kin seemed to outweigh all
other loyalties in the peasant Italians' code of honor.

So it was that, when transplanted to a New World,
Italians sought to preserve the strong family ties they
had known. Aided by the intensity of their tradition,
they succeeded in part in doing so. Even today other
Americans marvel at the closeness of Italian-American
families' relations. It is a trait that displays itself in the
gaiety of large family gatherings on birthdays and hol-
idays and also in the consolation it provides in times
of trouble and unhappiness.

Yet, neither the family institution nor any other as-
pect of the cultural traditions the immigrants brought
with them could remain entirely unaffected by the
New World environment. Commonly the second generation—the children of the immigrants—reflected the
changes being wrought. By the 1920s, for example,
many Italian-American newspapers were carrying
more and more features in English, in the hope of
maintaining the interest and support of a younger generation of more Americanized readers. By then, too,
many of the original immigrants were lamenting the
weaker sense of family solidarity exhibited by their
offspring. Some of the elders may have regretted, too,
that a different and more American kind of folk hero
was emerging among the youngsters. For while all

Italians continued to take pride in the renown of their artists—the opera stars Enrico Caruso and Amelita Galli-Curci, for example—perhaps the second generation was inclined to pay even more attention to the exploits of movie stars like Rudolph Valentino and All-American baseball players like Frank Crosetti and Tony Lazerri.

Change, and adjustment to American conditions, were evident too in the manner in which Italian-Americans increasingly resorted to the kinds of self-help that the Irish had utilized earlier. In part because of their unfamiliarity with the idea of labor organization, and in part because of the discrimination practiced against them by other workmen, Italian-Americans played little part in the American labor movement at first. But as they moved up in increasing numbers to better organized occupations—such as the needle trades in New York City's clothing industry—they demonstrated their willingness to participate actively in the unions' efforts to improve the lot of workers. Gradually their spokesmen, such as Luigi Antonini of the International Ladies' Garment Workers' Union, attained prominence in the ranks of nationally recognized leaders of labor.

In politics, the initial apathy among Italian-Americans bred by a lack of experience in public affairs in their old country also gradually melted away as they became more familiar with the power of the vote. In the late nineteenth and early twentieth centuries Italian-Americans tended to be Republicans. In part this was because many of the local Democratic organizations in cities where Italian immigrants settled were dominated by Irish bosses, who were reluctant to share their power with the still newer arrivals. In addition the Republican Party, which called itself the party of "the full dinner pail," attracted many New Immigrant votes in national elections because it supported high tariffs which supposedly protected the wages of American workmen.

Thus it was that some of the first Italian-Americans to achieve prominence in politics began their careers as Republicans. One of them was Fiorello La Guardia, who won fame as a Congressman in the 1920s and during his long term as Mayor of New York City (1934–1945). Other well-known Italian-American Republicans have been Edward Corsi, formerly federal commissioner of immigration, and John A. Volpe, who was twice elected Governor of Massachusetts in the 1960s.

As the voting strength of Italian-Americans grew, however, Irish Democratic politicians in many localities became more anxious to court their favor. During the 1920s Italian-Americans, and Catholics and immigrants in general, were under attack by the Ku Klux Klan and other extreme nativist groups. In those years in particular the Democrats in many cities and states made gains among New Immigrant voters by defending them against their detractors. When the Democrats nominated Al Smith for President in 1928, Italian-Americans and other minority group voters flocked to his support because he was a champion of tolerance.

Since that time Italian-Americans have played an increasing role in Democratic Party leadership.

Among the prominent figures they have produced are Charles Poletti, who served as Lieutenant Governor of New York during the 1930s; Carmine de Sapio, who was leader of New York's Tammany Hall during the 1950s; Governors Michael di Salle of Ohio and Albert Rossellini of Washington; Congressmen Peter Rodino and Hugh Addonizio of New Jersey; John O. Pastore, United States Senator from Rhode Island; and Anthony Celebreze, Secretary of Health, Education and Welfare in the cabinets of Presidents Kennedy and Johnson.

Regardless of party, however, Italian-American lawmakers have shown a notable tendency to support labor and welfare measures beneficial to the working class from which most of them sprang. They too, like the Catholic Irish, have helped bring about the emergence of modern America's liberal society.

If labor unionism and politics at first seemed strange to the earliest generation of Italian immigrants, so too did the emphasis which American society placed on education. School facilities for the lower classes had been totally inadequate in large parts of Italy; many immigrants had had no formal education at all. Consequently, some of them viewed American educational requirements as an unnecessary postponement of the day when the son or daughter might help contribute to the support of the family as a breadwinner. There was a suspicion also that the school might be a force which would compete with the family for the loyalty of its children. Nonetheless, the requirements were there on the lawbooks, and truant officers enforced them. As awareness grew that education pro-

vided a key for entry into better jobs and into the
professions, skepticism regarding its value declined
even among the most conservative members of the
older generation. By 1940 10 per cent of the freshmen
entering Columbia University, for example, were of
Italian descent.

There was some reason for the oldsters' fear that exposure to American conditions might challenge the
youngsters' loyalty to their inherited culture. Among
Italian-Americans, as among other ethnic minority
groups, that exposure sometimes produced a violent
reaction among second-generation individuals against
the "old-fashioned," "foreign," and "un-American"
ways of their elders. Taunted by the "native" Americans they met in school or in their jobs, they might re-
volt against parental authority, against their parents'
native language, against their religion and customs,
perhaps even against their family name. These reactions were particularly marked in periods when there
were strong pressures in American society demanding
conformity to a narrow definition of "100 per cent
Americanism"—as there were, for instance, in the
1920s. Such revolts frequently caused much bitterness
and frustration, both for the guardians of the minority
group's older traditions and for their children anxious
to parade a shallow kind of "Americanism."

For the minority groups as a whole, however, total
rejection of the immigrants' heritage by the later generations was not the most common response. Nor was it
usually permanent even among the rebels. For the
Italian-Americans, the worst of the conflict between
generations was over by the time of the Second World

War. By then many valuable parts of Italian culture had been adapted to American conditions, and Italian-Americans in all walks of life had proven beyond doubt the group's ability to contribute to the betterment of American society.

Thus Arturo Toscanini was recognized to be without peer among musical conductors, while Italian-Americans seemed to dominate the fields of opera and the plastic arts. The poet John Ciardi and the novelist Pietro di Donato were only two who stood high among American men of letters. The Italian-Americans could count thousands of doctors and lawyers, while outstanding jurists like Judges Ferdinand Pecora, Salvatore A. Cotillo, and John J. Freschi presided over federal and state courts. Italian-Americans now frequently owned the construction companies that their parents or grandparents had once dug ditches for, and they were prominent in many other industries as well. Giuseppe Bellanca was a famous airplane designer, for example, and the Giannini brothers controlled one of the country's most important banking firms. All America laughed at the comedy of Jimmy Durante; singers like Frank Sinatra and Perry Como rivaled even Bing Crosby in popularity; while many Americans considered Joe di Maggio the greatest "Yankee" of them all! And an Italian-American Nobel Prize winner, physicist Enrico Fermi, had helped introduce the world to a new age by his work in developing the atomic bomb.

By the 1940s, then, it was unlikely that a social worker would report—as one did earlier in the century —that "This family is not yet Americanized; they are still eating Italian food." By that time, indeed, the pizza or "tomato pie" was challenging the hot dog for first place as the typical American food. Few there were among Americans of Italian descent who failed to take pride in their heritage and in their group's contribution to the enrichment of American society and culture. Some later-generation descendants of immigrants who had passed up the opportunity to learn Italian at home now even paid money for instruction in the language of their fathers!

The contribution of Italian-Americans and other New Immigrant groups to the development of the United States stands in stark contradiction of the lament of the "native" American writer who, at the beginning of the twentieth century, complained that immigration after 1880 consisted of

> multitudes of men of the lowest class from the south of Italy and men of the meanest sort out of Hungary and Poland, men out of the ranks where there was neither skill nor energy nor any initiative of quick intelligence . . . as if the countries of the South of Europe were disburdening themselves of the more sordid and hapless elements of the population.

Yet his pessimistic attitude gained increasing support among the "natives" of his day to such an extent that, in the 1920s, they wrote into our immigration laws drastic discriminatory restrictions aimed against the New Immigrants—discriminations of a type that only the allegedly inferior races of the Orient had known earlier. Italian-Americans, and all of us, should bear those unfounded fears of the early twentieth century in mind as, today. we ponder the future and proper treatment of those ethnic minorities which still exist among *us.*

IV. IMMIGRATION EXCLUSION: THE CHINESE AND JAPANESE

EACH OF THE IMMIGRANT MINORITY GROUPS that came to America in the nineteenth century encountered opposition because of the threat its members allegedly posed to the jobs and the wage standards of older settlers. Each of them also suffered discrimination because their cultural characteristics differed in varying degrees from those of the "natives." But after the Civil War a third sort of discrimination—based on alleged racial differences—was added to the two mentioned above and applied to immigrants coming from the Orient.

Ideas about racial superiority and inferiority were not entirely new in America, of course. Before the Civil War many Southerners defended the institution of slavery on grounds of the supposed innate inferiority of the Negro race. After the Confederacy was defeated, white Southerners employed that argument even more fervently than ever, in the hope of persuading the victorious North to abandon radical reconstruction. At about the same time, agitators on the West Coast who were eager to discriminate against immigrants from China adopted similar arguments based on the alleged inherent inferiority of the yellow (Mongoloid) race.

At first the racial argument was applied only to Chinese, Japanese, and other Oriental immigrants. But eventually "natives" in other parts of the country began to entertain similar notions about the supposed racial inferiority of the Italian, Polish, Jewish and other New Immigrant groups—which weren't really "races" at all. Nevertheless, the tide of racist thinking gained momentum in the United States after the twentieth century began. Its influence helps account not only for the severity of the immigration restriction laws adopted in the 1920s but also particularly for the discriminatory bias evident in the manner in which those laws awarded immigration quotas among the different peoples of the world.

The Chinese were the first immigrants from the Far East to begin arriving in appreciable numbers. A trickle of them came at the time of the California Gold Rush of 1849. In the 1850s and 1860s much larger groups came to work on the railroads and in the mines then being developed in the American West. By 1880 there were more than a hundred thousand Chinese in the United States, the great bulk of them concentrated in California.

During the depression that began in 1873, jobs became scarce for settlers of all sorts who had poured into the West during the previous boom. In an effort to cut down on the supply of labor, white American workmen were soon agitating against the Chinese minority. (Ironically enough, many of the nativist leaders—such as Dennis Kearney—were Irish-Americans, whose cousins back East were still considered an undesirable minority element by most Yankees.) It was natural that these "natives" should turn against their Oriental competitors the economic arguments customarily employed against immigrant groups at the bottom of the occupational ladder. The Chinese were willing to work for extremely low "coolie" wages, they complained, and thus they deprived American working men of job opportunities.

It was natural, too, that the "natives" should ridicule the Chinamen's culture—their language, religions, customs, and traditions—and assert that their cultural differences made them unfit to become good Americans. After all, the same thing had been said, and would be said, about Germans, Irishmen, Italians, Jews and many other minority groups in other times or places.

But in addition, the Chinese *were* members of a different *race*, as well, set off from the whites (Caucasians) by color and physical appearance. Hence there was a strong temptation to account for the Chinamen's "undesirableness" on racial as well as economic and cultural grounds. The "backward" and "foreign" and "inferior" ways of the Chinese, native racists soon asserted, were passed on from generation to generation through the bloodstream of the yellow race. Consequently, they *could not* be erased or reformed or improved. The Chinese *could not* be assimilated. They *could not* "Americanize." They were incapable of contributing anything worthwhile to the American way of life. In fact, if their growth and influence went unchecked, it was contended, they would undermine the way of life followed by the American (white) race. Their further immigration must, therefore, be ended, and those already here must be held perpetually in an inferior status.

Such are the major ingredients of the racist argument when it is used against any ethnic minority. It had been and would for long be used successfully against America's Negroes. Now it was used successfully against Orientals.

From the outset the Chinese were handicapped in their attempts to fight back against the libels and discrimination to which they were subjected. A law passed in 1790 had limited the right to become naturalized citizens of the United States to "free white persons." At the time that provision had been aimed at slaves and at Indians living in tribal organizations. But now, in the 1870s, Western nativists contended that it applied to the Chinese as well. In 1878 a federal district court in California agreed with this interpretation. Thereafter Chinese immigrants were generally considered ineligible for citizenship (although any children born to them in America were, of course, native-born citizens).

At the same time, the natives stepped up their drive to end immigration from China altogether. Making full use of economic, cultural, and racial arguments, they gradually won enough support throughout the nation to have Congress pass, in 1882, a law which suspended Chinese immigration. That law, moreover, officially affirmed the ineligibility of Chinese immigrants already here to become naturalized citizens.

The Chinese Exclusion Act of 1882 marked an important turning point in American history. For the first time the potential value of persons wishing to come here was judged not on their individual merits but on their place of origin. It represented a sharp break with the nation's traditional attitudes—a break that was destined to grow in the years to come.

In addition to these official marks of "inferiority" imposed on them by federal law, Chinese settlers (and other Oriental minorities) in the United States tasted discrimination to a degree far exceeding that meted out to most other immigrant minorities coming from Europe. Cities and states in the West passed numerous laws that restricted their economic and social opportunities. In many places intermarriage (miscegenation) between Orientals and members of other races was forbidden. Frequently they were refused service in hotels, restaurants, and other public facilities. Their ability to move to better housing, even when they became able to afford it, was handicapped by restrictive covenants, whereby landlords refused to rent or sell to Orientals. Crowded Chinatowns were often subjected to criminal violence. In September 1885, for example, rioters in Rock Springs, Wyoming, murdered twenty-eight Chinese and destroyed property worth $148,000. Similar outbreaks were a common occurrence in other Western states. So were lynchings. Perhaps only the Negro can appreciate fully the humiliation and terror which Asian immigrants were made to suffer.

In such a hostile environment it was natural that the Chinese should seek comfort among their own kind, to an even greater extent than other immigrant groups.

The Chinese family—close-knit like the Italian's, to begin with—preserved much of its unity in the New World setting. In their restricted neighborhoods the immigrants constructed virtually self-contained communities, where Chinese doctors delivered Chinese babies, to be buried years later by Chinese undertakers. They built their own places of worship, and many large West Coast cities soon had Chinese theaters and Chinese newspapers. The immigrants also organized numerous fraternal and social societies, devoted to preserving their ancient culture and arts.

All this resembled the normal early development pattern of other immigrant groups, as we have seen. Yet in the case of the Chinese the persistence and thoroughness of their separateness was owing to something more than a mere desire for fellow-feeling on their own part. Segregation was *thrust* upon them and enforced by a dominant majority which was unwilling to have contact with them on any terms of equality and mutual respect. Their Chinatowns became virtual ghettoes from which there was no outlet, even if one desired to escape. Chinese bought and sold with other Chinese because there was no one else with whom to do business. Chinese limited themselves to Chinese entertainments and Chinese restaurants because they were not wanted elsewhere. Thus the Chinese were almost totally cut off from broader contacts with American life—even when they ardently desired them—by the will of the dominant majority. They *could not* Americanize because the natives would not give them the opportunity to do so. They *could not* assimilate because the natives chose to segregate them. They

could not contribute much to American life and culture because the natives refused to accept their gifts.

Thus the mutual give-and-take which gradually
made Irish-Americans out of Irish immigrants and
Italian-Americans out of Italian immigrants (and en-
riched American culture in the process) worked far
less effectively in the case of the Chinese. The traditional avenues whereby immigrant minority groups
gradually earned recognition and respect and
fulfillment were for the most part closed to them. Labor unions barred them from membership, for example; indeed, many West Coast labor organizations
were in the forefront among the Chinamen's oppres-
sors. Denied the right to become naturalized citizens,
the Chinese immigrants were thus denied the right to
vote; hence politicians need pay no heed to either
their material or psychological needs. True, the native-
born children of the immigrants could vote, but once
further immigration was cut off after 1882, the number
of these second-generation Chinese-Americans seemed
destined to remain so small as to make them impotent
as a political force.

Educational opportunities *were* open to the Chinese
and many, particularly among the second generation,
took advantage of them. Yet with few exceptions, for
the Chinese even the acquisition of education, experience, craftsmanship, and professional skills proved to
be only another road to frustration. An individual
might rise to prominence within his own Chinatown,
but rarely could he do so in the outside world that was
America. No matter how well prepared he was, the
Chinaman who aspired to a better position or career

usually found the way blocked by the bars of racial discrimination. Through education he might erase whatever personal or cultural defects he had, but he could not erase his color, his physical appearance, his race. He was a marked man for life, because the natives had decreed him a member of an inferior race from the start.

By the early twentieth century, then, native Americans had taught the Chinese "their place"—much as the Negroes had been taught "their place" earlier. The Chinese might find jobs as domestic servants, or as laundrymen, or doing other menial chores that catered to the needs of the white race. Or they might operate restaurants and curio shops and museums in Chinatown, to be patronized by tourists. But generally speaking that was about as far as their ambitions were permitted to go. The Chinese had been effectively excluded from competing with native Americans in most occupations and professions and in politics, just as they had been effectively excluded, by segregation, from social contacts with the outside world.

As the proportion of Chinese in America's total population declined year after year after 1900, many foresaw a time when there would be no evidence left at all to indicate that Chinese had ever emigrated to the United States and helped in its building. Thus it appeared that the minority problem—as far as the Chinese minority was concerned—was being solved in a way far different from the experience of the Irish, the Italians, and other immigrant groups. But that solution meant much greater hardship and heartbreak for the members of the minority group involved. And

as we can see today, it also involved a great loss for
America as a whole, in terms both of what the centu-
ries-old Chinese culture, and individual Chinese-Americans, might have contributed to this nation's enrichment had the natives only allowed them to do so.

Hardly had the West Coast nativists succeeded in
suppressing the Chinese when, at the turn of the century, the alleged menace of the "Yellow Peril" reap-
peared in the form of the increasing number of immigrants coming from Japan. In 1890 there were only 2,-
637 Japanese in America. But as population pressures
grew in the Land of the Rising Sun, more immigrants
made their way to the United States. By 1910 there
were about thirty thousand here, and by 1920 there
were approximately seventy-two thousand. Nearly 75
per cent of the Japanese resided in California, and
most of the rest settled in the two other West Coast
states of Washington and Oregon.

Once again native workmen feared that their jobs
and wage levels were in danger, as they complained of
the low living standards of their new competitors from
abroad. Ready made, too, for use against the Japanese
were the arguments concerning cultural differences
and alleged racial inferiority that had been employed
so successfully against the Chinese. Powerful labor
unions in San Francisco and elsewhere, and many employers, discriminated against the Japanese when they
sought any jobs above the most menial. Landlords and
operators of public facilities discriminated too. Sensa-
tion-seeking newspapers kept before the public eye
the alleged mongrelization of the white race which the

"Yellow Peril" supposedly represented. So did organizations like the Native Sons of the Golden West and the Asiatic Exclusion League.

In the fall of 1906 a government agency—the San Francisco Board of Education—entered the anti-Japanese campaign by ordering that all of the city's Japanese children be segregated in a separate school. This official act of discrimination caused the Japanese government to lodge strong protests in Washington, and President Theodore Roosevelt was sorely dismayed by the school board's action. Yet the board refused to back down. To appease it, the President negotiated the so-called gentlemen's agreement with Japan, whereby the Japanese government agreed to prohibit the further emigration of Japanese laborers to America. Only then did the board suspend its segregation order.

But the school board had won a tremendous victory for the West Coast nativists and racists. Following the gentlemen's agreement, Japanese immigration was reduced to a trickle. In 1924 it was shut off altogether. For the law of Congress that established quotas for immigrants from Europe that year excluded Japanese, Chinese, and other Orientals from admission to the United States. It also reaffirmed the ineligibility of Asian immigrants already here to become naturalized citizens.

While Japanese settlers in the cities were being effectively barred from securing desirable jobs in the early twentieth century, restrictions were also placed on the large number of them who had turned to agriculture. In their native country the Japanese had be-

come used to applying intensive farming techniques—
and investing huge amounts of back-breaking labor—
to small plots of poor soil. By using the same methods
in California they were able to turn marginal land into
veritable gardens—specializing in the production of
vegetables, flowers, and other hard-to-grow crops.
Even nativist newspapers sometimes praised the skill
with which the hard-working Japanese excelled in cul-
tivating difficult areas. Yet their success seemed only
to heighten the jealousy of the natives. In 1913 the
California legislature passed an Alien Land Act
which, in effect, forbade Japanese immigrants to own
land in the state. The Japanese found ways to evade
this discriminatory legislation to some extent (for example, it did not apply to Japanese children born in
America, who were, of course, native-born citizens of
the United States). Nevertheless, California's land
laws stood as another official mark of the Japanese immigrants' inferior status. So did the state law which
forbade the issuance of commercial fishing licenses to
Japanese immigrants who had settled in seacoast cities
and towns.

Whether they resided in the cities or the countryside, then, the Japanese found themselves hemmed in
by the walls of discrimination. Especially affected
were the second-generation Japanese-Americans. They
were citizens, but found themselves suspended between the culture of their parents, which in many
ways seemed foreign to them, and the culture of native Americans, who rejected them on racial grounds.
The attempts of these native-born Nisei (pronounced
nee-say) to prove their Americanism sometimes caused

painful conflict with the first-generation Issei (pronounced *ees-say*). Many Nisei drifted away from the Oriental religions of their fathers, for example, and converted to Christianity. More than many other second-generation immigrant groups, moreover, the Nisei eagerly seized the opportunities for schooling that America provided. Sometimes this conflicted with the first generations' preference to educate their children in Japanese-type schools. The Nisei were extremely active also in forming organizations—sports, religious, cultural, civic, fraternal, and social groups. One study in 1939 counted at least 486 Nisei organizations active on the West Coast.

Yet the frequency with which Japanese-American citizens founded such organizations reflected the fact that, generally speaking, non-Japanese groups were not open to them. Regardless of their education or other personal qualities, individual Nisei—like Chinese, Negroes, and other victims of racial discrimination—found social contact with native white Americans difficult to achieve. Moreover, the paths toward advancement that European immigrants used—better jobs, unionization, and effective political pressure, for example—were also beyond the reach of these members of the yellow race.

So it was that by 1940 the great majority of Japanese immigrants and Japanese-Americans remained employed as farm laborers, fish-cannery workers, or as domestic servants and in personal service trades in the cities. "Little Tokyos" existed in some of the larger West Coast cities, and the ambitious Japanese-American might hope to achieve some local prominence as a business or professional man there among his own people. But the walls of the ghetto limited his ambitions, and with few exceptions forbade him to aspire to any wider recognition among other Americans.

Year by year the proportion of Japanese to the total American population declined. It appeared, then, that like the Chinese, the Japanese might soon become an extinct element, leaving hardly any traces behind in the history of American ethnic minority groups.

Still one more indignity remained to be heaped on the Japanese in America before their humiliation was complete, however. As diplomatic relations between the United States and Japan grew worse during the late 1930s, distrust of the Japanese who were congregated on the West Coast, often near naval and other defense installations, grew. After Japan's attack on Pearl Harbor on December 7, 1941, that suspicion knew no bounds. Acting on the advice of military authorities, President Franklin D. Roosevelt in the spring of 1942 approved an order for the removal of the Japanese away from the coastal areas. Altogether 110,-000 Japanese were uprooted from their homes and sent to ten relocation camps inland. Of that number 40,000 were alien immigrants, but fully 70,000 were native-born citizens. No similar steps were taken against German and Italian aliens in this country during the war, let alone against German-American and Italian-American *citizens*. Nevertheless, even the Supreme Court of the United States upheld the constitutionality of the removal order, largely on the grounds of military necessity. A distinguished law professor wrote later:

> The evacuation of Japanese-Americans from the Pacific Coast . . . was an act without precedent in American history. It was the first time that the United States government condemned a large group of people to barbed-wire enclosures. It was the first event in which danger to the nation's welfare was determined by group characteristics rather than by individual guilt. It was the first program in which. race alone determined whether an American would remain free or become incarcerated.

It was, we might add, the culmination of the long string of abuses which race-conscious native Americans had heaped upon members of the yellow racial minorities.

Yet it may turn out that the Second World War marked an important turning point in the history of America's Oriental ethnic minorities. For one thing, the labor shortage which it created on the home front lowered some of the employment barriers that had kept members of non-white races out of better jobs. During the war years Chinese-Americans were able to secure work in aircraft assembly plants and in other factories, as office clerks, and in many other lines formerly reserved for whites only. Even some Japanese-Americans were sent from the relocation camps to fill similar positions in labor-shortage areas across the country. This new degree of occupational mobility was also accompanied by a greater degree of geographical mobility as Orientals began to disperse throughout the nation. Thereafter the Chinatowns and Little Tokyos no longer bound the lives and the ambitions of Asian-Americans to the extent that they had before.

Moreover, China was an ally of the United States in the war against the Axis powers; it hardly seemed fair and honorable to continue persecution at home against immigrants from a country whose armies fought side by side with our own. Meanwhile, the brilliant record made in the fighting in Europe by the 442nd Regimental Combat Team—composed of second-generation Japanese-American volunteers—proved conclusively the full-blooded loyalty of the Japanese-American minority group.

In the postwar years, then, most native Americans demonstrated a friendlier attitude toward Chinese-Americans than had been customary. Many of them were ashamed, too, of the outrage that the relocation of the Japanese represented, and efforts were made by the federal government to repay financial losses that the Japanese had suffered as a result of it. All this was reflected in a lessening of the official marks of discrimination against Orientals as well. After the end of the war, for example, federal courts declared California's Alien Land Law, and that state's discriminatory law against alien Japanese fishermen, to be unconstitutional. In 1950 Congress passed a bill enabling the alien Japanese immigrants then living in the United States to become naturalized citizens. During the war the

Chinese Exclusion Act of 1882 was repealed, and China was awarded a token immigration quota of 105 persons annually. In the McCarran-Walter Immigration Act of 1952 China, Japan, and other Asian countries were given at least small quotas, and thus the stigma of absolute exclusion was removed from them. The same act also removed the ban against Orientals becoming naturalized citizens.

Still one other development contributed to brighten the prospects of Oriental minorities in the United States. In 1950, as colonialism tumbled throughout the world, Hawaii was admitted to the Union as our fiftieth state. Her population embraces a more varied mixture of ethnic stocks than any other American state; more than one-third of her people are of Chinese or Japanese descent. The citizens of the new state promptly sent to Washington, as one of their first United States Senators, Hiram L. Fong, a Chinese-American. To represent them in the House of Representatives they chose Daniel K. Inouye, an American of Japanese ancestry. As a result, Asian-Americans had achieved a degree of political recognition and representation that was far beyond their reach earlier.

Since the end of the Second World War access to better jobs, to the professions, and to opportunities in all walks of life has become easier for members of the Oriental minorities. A Chinese-American, James Wong Howe, has won recognition as one of the world's great motion-picture photographers; Sessue Hayakawa and Sono Osato, Japanese-Americans, are stars of Hollywood who might appear before his lenses. Artists such as Dong Kingman, a Chinese-American, and Japanese-

American Isamu Noguchi have won national acclaim for their work in painting and sculpture. All Americans took pride when Chinese-Americans Tsung Dao Lee and Chen-Ning Yang, professors at Princeton and Columbia, shared the Nobel Prize in Physics in 1957. A year earlier the students of Michigan State University had voted Dr. Anthony Koo, Professor of Economics, their most distinguished teacher of the year.

Even more than before, young Asian-Americans eagerly seek to further their schooling; today the educational level of second-generation Japanese-Americans stands considerably above the national average. Still more to the point is the fact that the efforts and sacrifices of Chinese-American citizens like Joseph Lin Gong, whose five children are graduates of Harvard, Florida State University, Wellesley College, Purdue, and the University of New Hampshire, are not as likely, now, to be frustrated by walls of blind racial discrimination. Indeed in 1947 Joseph Lin Gong's oldest son, Eddie, was chosen as the American Legion's "Boy President of the U. S. A."

So, at long last, it appears that Chinese- and Japanese-Americans, and other Asian immigrant groups, may be allowed the opportunities that ethnic minorities from Europe have enjoyed. As a result, individuals from Oriental minority groups will be enabled to take fuller advantage of the chances for self-improvement that America provides. At the same time, they will be more able to contribute, out of the culture of their ancient civilizations, to the enrichment of America's own way of life.

The extent to which these developments take place

will provide evidence of the extent to which native white Americans have overcome one of the most insidious forms of ethnic discrimination and prejudice—that based upon supposedly inherent racial inferiority. Eradication of racism from American thinking cannot come too soon. In the past it has not only brought particular heartbreak for Chinese-Americans, Japanese-Americans, and the other non-white minorities against whom it was directed with full force. For as mentioned at the beginning of this chapter, the racist doctrines leveled first against American Negroes and then against immigrants from the Orient in the late nineteenth century were also applied, to some extent, against the New Immigration from Europe in the early twentieth century. Those doctrines made a deep imprint on the general immigration restriction legislation adopted in the 1920s—an imprint which still survived even in the McCarran-Walter Immigration Act of 1952.

V. IMMIGRATION RESTRICTION AND AN EXCEPTION: THE PUERTO RICANS

WHILE PACIFIC COAST AGITATORS were busy erecting barriers against the bearers of the so-called "Yellow Peril" in the early years of the twentieth century, a growing number of native Americans elsewhere in the country concluded that the time had come to end the liberal policy toward European immigration that had prevailed since the days of Washington and Jefferson. From the 1890s onward the American Federation of Labor and other native-dominated unions, concerned about the alleged oversupply of labor, campaigned in favor of imposing a numerical limit on annual immigration. At the same time other "natives" determined that steps were necessary to preserve the "real American" way of life, which they identified with the culture of British-American colonial settlers and those Old Immigrant groups that had most easily assimilated to it. Their arguments were reinforced by a growing tendency to describe the more different and New Immigrant nationality stocks as races, whose inherently "inferior" ways of life were supposedly transmitted from generation to generation with no possibility of elevation or improvement.

Thus in 1911 a group that had been directed by Congress to study immigration and the adjustment of immigrants to America—the Dillingham Commission —presented statistics which identified the Irish and the New Immigrant nationalities with higher-than-average rates of poverty, crime, vice, poor health, drunkenness, and mental illness. The commission's report tended to blame these conditions on the "racial characteristics" of the Newer American nationality groups involved rather than on the *environmental* handicaps which they commonly endured—low pay, poor housing, and social discrimination. Later, many of the commission's findings were exploded as being pure myths. For the time being, however, they lent support to the nativist prejudice that American culture was threatened not only by a Yellow Peril but also by a general foreign peril as well.

The First World War and its aftermath further stimulated the growth of nativism. The war effort generated demands for undivided conformity to something called "100 per cent Americanism"; the suspicion of foreign things that resulted became almost hysterical. When the war ended many feared that an economic depression was in store; the demand that jobs be conserved for returning veterans fortified the argument that competition from a new flood of immigrants should be ended through numerical restriction. At the same time, following the Russian Communist Revolution of late 1917, a gigantic Red scare swept the United States. Many tended to identify the Communist threat to American institutions with the immigrants from southern and eastern Europe who were again seeking refuge on our shores in large numbers.

Finally, it is true that wartime conditions, and then increased urbanization and technological advances, fostered a revolution in American manners and moral standards of behavior in the decade after 1917. Much of the Puritan strain in American life was weakened during the 1920s. Many Protestant old-stock Americans—particularly those who lived in rural and small-town areas—were greatly disturbed by these far-reaching changes. But rather than recognizing them as products of the vast environmental and psychological transformations that were taking place in the country, many old-stock natives blamed the influence of the cultural or racial characteristics of the Irish and New Immigrant masses who inhabited the great cities of the nation. The "real America" must be preserved from the corrupting influence of these Newer American minority groups, they claimed.

So it was that, in a series of laws enacted during the 1920s, Congress for the first time imposed a limit, of approximately 157,000, on the number of immigrants who might be admitted each year. (This contrasted with the figure of 1,285,349 who were admitted in 1907 alone.) Moreover, the total number of admissions was divided up into quotas, assigned to various nations of the world *supposedly* on the basis of what each had contributed, since 1607, to the ethnic make-up of "the American nationality" as it existed in 1920. Consequently, the countries of northern and western Europe, whose immigrants had come earliest and in the largest numbers, received by far the largest quotas.

More than two-fifths of the available 157,000 places went to Great Britain, for example, despite the fact that few Britons now desired to come to America; as a result her quota has never been fully used. By contrast the countries of the New Immigration, whose people had not begun to come here in large numbers until the 1880s, received very small quotas. Only 5,666 Italians could be admitted each year, for example, and only 6,488 Poles. As mentioned earlier, China, Japan, and other Asian countries were especially discriminated against, for no quotas at all were allotted to them.

The closing of America's traditional open door to immigrants naturally implied an unfavorable judgment upon those American citizens, *already here,* whose homelands received very small quotas. During the 1920s groups like the Ku Klux Klan and other nativist elements undertook to limit the supposedly unhealthy influence which parts of the citizenry—be they Catholics, Jews, Negroes, the Irish, the New Immigrants, or just "foreigners" in general—exerted in American life. Prohibition and other "blue laws" sought to curb their "immoral" habits. In some states efforts were made to outlaw parochial schools. When in 1928 Al Smith—a spokesman for the urban, industrial, immigrant New America—aspired to become President, nativists rallied to put down the menace which he allegedly posed to traditional Old American values.

Thus, by the 1920s, America had learned that the melting pot did not really melt away all ethnic differences—and indeed it never had worked that way. Awaking to that fact, some old-stock native Americans

—who claimed to "own" the country—undertook to define the real American nationality. Their definition generally identified America as a white Anglo-Saxon Protestant civilization—and thus they defined Americanism in terms of characteristics that were identical with their own. During the 1920s they sought to enforce conformity to their standards and to deny first-class citizenship to those whom they thought could never meet them. Theirs was the "superior" way of life, and they reshaped the nation's immigration laws in an attempt to keep it predominant.

The era of the melting pot was over. An era of narrow nationalism, and of forced conformity to a narrow definition of 100 per cent Americanism, seemed to be at hand.

The immigration bars that were clamped down during the 1920s were, nonetheless, not totally effective in preventing new and, in the eyes of nativists, inferior ethnic groups from entering the country. For reasons based on the objectives of American foreign policy, for example, no quotas were imposed upon immigration from countries in the Western Hemisphere. Consequently, groups such as the French-Canadians continued to immigrate in search of jobs in New England textile mills, while Mexicans crossed the southern border to work as migratory farm laborers in our Western states. People from these groups who settled permanently in the United States relived the same cycle of hardship and discrimination, but eventual advance and increasing self-fulfillment, that had been the history of the European immigrant groups of the nineteenth century.

But the most dramatic of the immigration movements by those exempt from the restrictive legislation of the 1920s has been that of the Puerto Ricans. Inhabitants of the Caribbean island acquired by the United States after the war with Spain in 1898, they were given full legal citizenship by a law of Congress passed in 1917. Consequently there are no limitations whatever on their freedom to enter the United States. They are as free to come and go to New York or Chicago as are citizens of Virginia or California. A trickle of them began to do so when, in the 1920s, restriction of European immigration seemed to open up more job opportunities, on the lower rungs of the occupational ladder, for the Puerto Ricans. Thereafter the poverty of existence on their own island, because of its limited natural resources and its exploding birth rate, stimulated the desire of many more Puerto Ricans to migrate to the mainland. The 1940 census reported nearly seventy thousand persons of Puerto Rican birth living in the continental United States. All but nine thousand of them congregated in New York City, where their main job market existed.

The ability of Puerto Ricans to fulfill their dreams of migration was greatly increased when, at the end of the Second World War, direct and low-cost air service was begun between New York and the island's capital city of San Juan. As a result, more than a million additional Puerto Ricans were added to the mainland population between 1945 and 1965. A minority of them, from the rural areas of the island, worked as seasonal farm hands in our Western states and on Eastern truck farms; these, following the summer harvest months, usually returned to Puerto Rico for the winter. But most of the immigrants flocked to New York City, although in more recent years a rising proportion of them have dispersed to other cities. Thus not only New York but Chicago, Philadelphia, Camden, Trenton, Bridgeport, Pittsburgh, San Francisco, Los Angeles, Detroit, Boston, Gary, Buffalo and Miami now have their distinctive Puerto Rican quarters.

Surely the Puerto Rican immigrants arriving aboard sleek airliners in the mid-twentieth century have had an easier time of it, in terms of their passage, than the earlier groups from Europe who voyaged for weeks in the holds of slow-moving ships. In terms of finding jobs, too, these newest immigrants enjoy types of public assistance that were unheard of in earlier times; the Migration Division of the Department of Labor of the Commonwealth of Puerto Rico, for instance, maintains employment offices in New York and other focal points. No longer need these modern-day immigrants rely, as the Italians before them, on a frequently grasping *padrone*.

Moreover, today's public-welfare agencies maintained by cities and states, and the Social Security system of the federal government, relieve the Puerto Rican settlers of many of the anxieties that plagued earlier settlers. To a much greater degree than his nineteenth-century predecessors, the Puerto Rican immigrant need not be dependent in times of adversity on a scheming political boss. In addition, having been raised in a Commonwealth of the United States, he is much more familiar than other immigrants were with American ideas, institutions, and political processes, as well as with the more material aspects of American life.

Despite all these advantages, the Puerto Rican nevertheless finds adjustment to his new surroundings difficult enough. Like earlier immigrants, he is usually poor, undereducated, and unskilled. Consequently he finds only the most menial and least-paying jobs open to him—as a laborer, janitor, dishwasher, or, at best, an unskilled factory hand. As a result, the Puerto Rican can usually afford only the least desirable housing accommodations—frequently in slum areas from which succeeding waves of earlier immigrants have graduated. In this frustrating environment the Puerto Ricans and their children encounter the same menaces to physical and mental health, and the same temptations to yield to crime, vice, and immorality, that Irishmen, Italians, and others whom they have displaced sometimes succumbed to.

Moreover, the Puerto Ricans' new neighbors find the presence of this latest wave of newcomers disturbing, just as they did the waves of Irishmen, Italians, and others who came earlier. Once again one hears the economic complaints of natives—among whom Irishmen, Italians, and members of other former minority groups now number—to the effect that Puerto Rican competition undercuts American working standards.

One also hears familiar complaints about the "foreignness" of the newcomers' culture. Since Spanish is still more or less the mother tongue and official language of Puerto Rico, many of her immigrants arrive here ignorant of English. Most of them are Catholics—a fact which disturbs some Protestants, although the Spanish-oriented type of Catholicism which the Puerto Ricans bring with them seems strange enough, too, to many native Catholics. The music and art, the habits and customs, and the foods native to Puerto Rico—all flavored by the island's essentially Spanish heritage—serve to increase the immigrants' visibility as a minority group in the American urban setting. The strangeness of it all in the eyes of the natives is increased by the fact that, since enactment of the immigration restriction laws of the 1920s, America *has* undoubtedly become a more homogeneous nation with a more uniform culture. We *are* less used to diversity than when, in the nineteenth century, our liberal immigration policies brought hundreds of thousands of strangers to our shores each year.

Finally, the matter of color and race also enters into the question of the Puerto Ricans' adjustment. Generally speaking, Puerto Ricans are of darker complexion than mainland white Americans. This is partly a result of the large degree of intermarriage that took place between the Spanish who settled the island long ago and the Negroes whom they imported to work on the sugar plantations. Some "white" Americans therefore consider all Puerto Ricans as being "colored"—which they are not. Or there is the tendency to speak of the Puerto Ricans as being members of a separate race—which they are not. Nonetheless, some present-day nativists continue to insist upon blaming whatever difficulties the Puerto Ricans encounter on their allegedly inferior and nonerasable racial characteristics rather than on the environmental handicaps which they, as a group, suffer.

Puerto Rican immigrants are subjected, therefore, to the kinds of economic and cultural discrimination that have been the lot of each succeeding group of European immigrants. They know to a considerable degree the even harsher form of racial discrimination which has been felt most directly by Negroes, the Chinese and Japanese, and other non-white minorities. Certainly this adds to the difficulties they must experience in attaining advancement and self-fulfillment as individuals and acceptance as a group.

As we have seen, other immigrant minority groups seeking to adjust to a frequently hostile environment have traditionally established networks of institutions and organizations designed to serve their own particular needs—churches, newspapers, cultural and social and fraternal societies of all kinds. Such institutions have not only served to comfort the alien first generation of immigrants, but also have usually provided the means whereby the second-generation children of the immigrants developed leadership for their group and moved more directly into the mainstream of American life. To some extent the Puerto Ricans have followed the same pattern.

Yet, in comparison with earlier immigrant groups, such activities and organizations do not seem to flourish so vigorously among the Puerto Ricans. Perhaps the greater availability of public agencies of assistance in times of need helps account for this fact. So too does the nearness of Puerto Rico and the ease with which the immigrant can return there temporarily or permanently if he wants to—all of which has perhaps tended to keep the Puerto Ricans' attention focused on their island homeland. Moreover, it is undoubtedly now more difficult than in the past to preserve distinct cultural heritages, owing to the widespread influence of television, radio, movies, and the other mass media.

Nevertheless the fears expressed by some—that the Puerto Ricans' relative lack of success in building an extensive system of self-help institutions within their own communities may hinder the development of leaders for their group—are most probably groundless. For already, without undergoing such an intense degree of inward organizational development as earlier immigrant groups experienced, the Puerto Ricans seem to be more directly utilizing the same avenues toward advancement and acceptance that each of the earlier minorities eventually traveled. The labor movement is more willing now than in the past to welcome these newest arrivals into its fold. Consequently, as Puerto Ricans move into jobs formerly dominated by Italians and Jews in the New York City needle trades, for example, they are being rapidly organized. Already Puerto Ricans occupy seats on the executive councils of the powerful garment-industry unions.

In politics, Democratic Party leadership in several areas of New York City has already passed from the hands of Italian-Americans to Puerto Ricans—just as it had passed earlier to the Italians from the Irish. In 1965 Herman Badillo, a native of Caguas, Puerto Rico, was elected Borough President of the Bronx. Puerto

Ricans also appear eager to make use of the expanded educational opportunities now more readily available to members of the lower economic class. As a result, their group is producing a growing number of professional men, businessmen, and educators—leaders who are anxious to bridge whatever gaps separate their people from the rest of the American population.

These spokesmen, familiar with American history and with the history of former minority groups, confidently expect the Puerto Ricans gradually to progress along the same path followed by the Irish, the Italians, and the others who preceded them. To over-anxious native Americans who criticize the island immigrants' failure to advance more rapidly than they have, these leaders make a telling reply. It is now only about twenty years, they point out, since the great impact of Puerto Rican immigration began to make itself felt on our shores. In the history of any American ethnic minority, that is indeed a short time. It means that the situation of the Puerto Ricans of today must be compared with the status of the Irish-Americans in the 1860s, of the Chinese-Americans in the 1880s, and of the Italian-Americans about 1900. If the Puerto Ricans are judged in those terms, their spokesmen contend, then this latest of our immigrant minority groups may be quite satisfied with its record. Objective observers must agree with that evaluation.

Given the short time that the Puerto Rican group has had to develop in the United States, it is understandable that most of its members who have attained well-known reputations—actors Jose Ferrer and Rita Moreno; concert pianist Jesus Maria Sanroma and

Metropolitan Opera star Justino Diaz; baseball stars Orlando Cepeda and Roberto Clemente, for example —have won their prominence in the fields of art, entertainment, and athletics. For traditionally those have been the roads to fame and fortune most open to minority groups with the least prejudice and discrimination. But if history is any guide, their fields of ambition and conquest will broaden, just as the horizons of Irish-Americans have broadened since the days of Paddy Ryan and John L. Sullivan. There is no reason to doubt that, with time and under proper conditions, Puerto Ricans will win recognition in every walk of life.

At least three requirements must be filled, however, if the traditional pattern is to be allowed to unfold for the Puerto Ricans and other present-day ethnic minority groups. The first is the maintenance of a dynamic, growing national economy, and one which takes due account of the importance of the human beings it serves. Only a growing economy can provide job opportunities enough to assure maximum employment at all levels for our total population. And only an economy sensitive to human values can make provision for the special needs of those like the Puerto Ricans who, being at the bottom of the occupational ladder, find themselves particularly threatened by special problems such as automation.

The second requirement must be a willingness and determination on the part of the Puerto Ricans themselves to make the sacrifices necessary to their own self-advancement within a dynamic, growing America.

They must realize, as their leaders do, that none of America's ethnic groups—beginning even with the British-Americans of colonial days—have had an easy time of it in realizing their own best potentialities. All have had to strive, sacrifice, and save—and to be satisfied with slow, often painful progress. And, coming as they do into a rapidly changing and highly technical, industrialized America, our newest immigrants perhaps face new obstacles and demands. In an era when a premium is placed upon skill and training in the job market, for example, the Puerto Ricans may very well have to put even greater emphasis upon the need for education than our nineteenth-century immigrants did.

The final requirement is perhaps the most important of all to meet. If the Puerto Ricans are to be enabled to contribute their full part to the building of America, then it will be necessary for the earlier arrivals—the native Americans—to overcome those prejudices which have in the past made the way more difficult than it need have been for the successive waves of strangers in the land. Even the most ambitious and hard-working Puerto Rican is doomed to unnecessary frustration if his efforts to contribute to his own and to the nation's improvement are broken on the rocks of economic, cultural, and racial discrimination.

Fortunately there are encouraging signs that the xenophobic and ethnocentric tendencies of the "natives" —tendencies which reached their peak during the "100 per cent American" mania of the 1920s—have been on the wane since the end of that decade. To the extent that they do give way to a broader and more tolerant concept of Americanism, the nation will be better able to profit from the many contributions which the Puerto Ricans and other present-day minority groups stand ready to make to its welfare.

Dreams of freedom and wealth lured many immigrants across the sea to America in the mid-19th century. *(Museum of the City of New York. Photograph by Lewis Hine)*

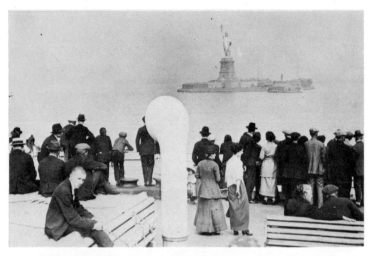

The Statue of Liberty greeted them, the symbol of hope for a better tomorrow. *(Culver Pictures)*

Immigrants were numbered and tagged in the railroad waiting room at Ellis Island. *(George Eastman House Collection. Photograph by Lewis Hine)*

Thousands settled in the crowded tenements of the lower East Side in New York. *(Brown Brothers)*

They had dreamed that the streets were paved with gold, but, in fact, hard labor, long hours and little pay were what they found. *(George Eastman House Collection. Photograph by Lewis Hine)*

Children formed friendships. *(George Eastman House Collection. Photograph by Lewis Hine)*

In the slums still existing in New York, children find places to play. *(Commonwealth of Puerto Rico)*

A cartoonist illustrates the hostilities faced by the Chinese immigrants on their arrival in San Francisco in the 1880s. *(Culver Pictures)*

One Nation Indivisible, 1942. Two days later the Army evacuated all persons of Japanese ancestry from the Pacific Coast. *(War Relocation Authority, Dorothea Lange)*

The Negroes, who came as involuntary immigrants, slaved in the fields of the South. *(Farm Security Administration. Photograph by Dorothea Lange)*

Even in the 20th century, the Negro's security continues to be threatened by the Ku Klux Klan. *(Rapho-Guillumette. Photograph by Bruce Roberts)*

In 1963 people of all races, religions and nationalities joined together in the March on Washington to demand equality for all. *(Magnum. Photograph by Bruce Davidson)*

VI. THE OLDEST MINORITY: NEGRO AMERICANS

As a rule, the farther back into American history a particular ethnic group can trace its roots, the less likely is it still to be considered a minority group today. But as with most rules, this one has at least one exception. The first Negroes landed in America a year before the Pilgrims disembarked at Plymouth, only a few years after the first permanent English settlement was established at Jamestown, and long before Catholic Irish, Italians, Orientals, or Puerto Ricans began to come here in any considerable numbers. Yet today, after three and a half centuries, Negroes constitute our oldest, largest, and most enduring minority group, and the problem of their situation is perhaps the most pressing and difficult domestic issue confronting the country at the present time.

It was in 1619 that a Dutch ship bound from Africa for the Spanish West Indies carrying a cargo of slaves was blown off course and put in at Jamestown. There twenty Negroes were sold to colonists who were in need of additional hands, and henceforth the slave ships made more regular calls in Virginia and the oth-

er English colonies that soon dotted the North American coast.

It appears that at first the Negroes were treated
much the same as the white indentured servants who
came from Europe and who sold themselves into servi-
tude for a period (usually seven years) in return for
their passage. But there was a vital difference, in addition to that of color, between the white and Negro immigrant servants. The whites came *voluntarily;* good
treatment on the part of their masters and strict hon-
oring of the terms of liberation specified in their contracts (indentures) were essential in their case in order to encourage a continuing flow of new voluntary
servants from Europe. The Negroes—captured or
bought by the slave traders along the coast of Africa—
were *involuntary* immigrants, on the other hand. They
had no ties or communication with those "back home";
they had no "advertising" value, therefore; and the
treatment they received could in no way affect the
supply of them. Consequently, their treatment degen-
erated and their periods of service lengthened, even as
the condition of the white indentured servant class
improved.

Finally, in 1664 the legislature of Maryland decreed
that all Negroes then in the colony were to be servants
for life by virtue of their color. Thereafter that condition was made hereditary and imposed on the offspring of Negroes. Other colonies followed suit. Slave
codes were enacted, and slavery became official in
America. The inferior social status of all Negroes, as a
group, was fixed in every detail. No other among our
many ethnic groups would ever be so completely de-

nied, *by law,* the opportunities for social mobility and individual advancement that America offered its inhabitants.

Slavery existed in all the American colonies prior to the Revolution, but after 1776 it was gradually abolished in the Northern states. In the South, on the other hand, the institution became more solidly entrenched as, during the first half of the nineteenth century, the cultivation of cotton and the plantation system became central to the South's economy and way of life. There is no need to rehearse here the injustice of slavery, or the contradiction that its persistence in a supposedly modern and democratic country represented. Nor need we dwell on the long trail of events whereby it led to the disruption of the Union. Suffice it to say that by 1860 the people of the North had determined —out of a mixture of humanitarian and self-interested motives—to put an end to the spread of the slave system. The result was the Civil War, a tragedy which almost resulted in the nation's undoing. At its end, however, slavery had been dealt a mortal blow. In the Thirteenth Amendment to the Constitution, adopted late in 1865, it was outlawed.

It should be remembered, however, that the abolition of slavery only made the Negroes freemen; it did not automatically determine what their exact status in society should be. Their position as slaves had been fixed by law; it would take new laws to determine their new condition. During 1865 and 1866 the Southern state governments established under the Lincoln–Johnson mild program of Reconstruction passed a series of Black Codes that severely restricted the rights of the freemen. Not until the so-called Radical Republicans assumed control of Congress in 1867, and added the Fourteenth Amendment to the Constitution, were the full rights of citizenship legally conferred on the nation's Negroes. In 1870 the Fifteenth Amendment forbade the states to deny any citizen the right to vote on the basis of race or color. During the next few years Radical Republican administrations in Washington and in the Southern states sought to protect and enforce the Negroes' citizenship and voting rights.

In carrying out their program to elevate the condition of the Negro, however, the Radicals sadly neglected his economic plight. Lacking that bedrock of economic security and independence in which true freedom of action must be rooted, the Negro was ill-prepared to defend his newly acquired political and social prerogatives against those Southern whites who were anxious to reassert their own supremacy and to relegate the Negro to something less than full equality. Incapable of adequate self-defense, the Negro found himself dependent upon the protection of the white North. Should the North's interest or determination concerning "the Southern question" wane, the Negro would find himself at the mercy of his former masters.

So it was that, with the passage of time in the 1870s, the people of the North turned their attention to other matters and lost the will to continue enforcement of the Radical Reconstruction program. (The spread of racist thinking at about the same time among some nativist elements in the North and West, as mentioned in an earlier chapter, also militated against the Southern

Negroes' cause.) After 1877 all of the Southern states were back in the hands of the "Redeemers," as the anti-Negro white Southerners called themselves, and soon the work of the "Restoration"—the restoration of white supremacy, that is to say—was under way.

To economic exploitation of the Negro the white South now added elaborate forms of social discrimination. One of them involved compulsory segregation of the races in public establishments and facilities. When the Supreme Court ruled in 1896 *(Plessy* v. *Ferguson)* that state segregation laws did not violate the Fourteenth Amendment, so long as the separate facilities were "equal," the extent of the federal government's abandonment of the Negro was substantially proven. The "separate but equal" doctrine thereafter gave the white South a green light to impose massive, all-pervasive segregation on the Negro element *by law,* as a mark of the whites' racial "superiority." Nor did anyone really bother to insure that the separate facilities provided for Negroes were in fact equal. In his dilapidated Jim Crow schools, railroad cars, hotels, stores, theaters, restaurants, rest rooms, and cemeteries, the Negro was reminded a hundred times daily of his racial "inferiority." A city ordinance of Birmingham, Alabama, even made it a criminal offense for "a Negro and a white person to play together or in company with each other at dominoes or checkers."

By 1900, moreover, the Southern states had also hit upon methods that effectively prevented most Negroes from exercising their right to vote. Poll taxes, literacy tests, and "white primary" laws (which defined political parties as private clubs, and thereby enabled them

to set membership rules that excluded colored persons
from voting in primary elections)—none of these de-
vices specifically mentioned race or color. Thus, it was
held, they did not violate the Fifteenth Amendment.
But in actual practice they sufficed virtually to eliminate Negro influence in Southern politics. In Louisi-
ana, for example, 130,000 Negroes were registered to
vote in 1896; in 1904, after the state had adopted some
of the discriminatory measures mentioned above, only
1,342 were eligible to cast ballots. Rare indeed, for
many years after the turn of the century, was the
Southern Negro who dared brave the barriers erected
by law against his exercise of the franchise. Since the
Democratic Party which now dominated the "Solid
South" ran only candidates who opposed racial justice
and equality, what use did there seem to be for Negroes to bother trying to vote at all?

Lacking a sound economic base for his own self-defense, deserted or ignored by the white North, subject
to the whim of white Southerners and to the legal
coercion of the state governments they controlled, the
Southern Negro by 1900 presented a forlorn figure. In
such circumstances, it was rather natural that many
Negroes should lapse into an attitude of acquiescence
bordering on subservience. A philosophy which
seemed to fit that mood was developed by Booker T.
Washington, a former slave who emerged in the late
nineteenth and early twentieth centuries as a leading
spokesman for Negro aspirations. Suggesting that for
the time being the Negro minority put aside agitation
for full political and social equality, Washington
urged his fellows to concentrate on developing voca-

tional education and acquiring work skills that would
enable them to improve their economic position. From
that platform, Washington believed, Negroes might
gradually convince the white man of their genuine
worth as productive citizens; thereafter, the white
majority might prove more willing to accord Negroes
the social and political rights that were due them.

It should be remembered that Washington did not
advocate *permanent* submission by the Negroes to
their condition of social and political inferiority. But
as time passed without alleviation of the burdens
inflicted on them, nagging questions wracked thoughtful Negroes and those relatively few whites who sym-
pathized with them. *How long* must the Negroes wait,
and *how often* must they prove their usefulness and
potential, before they might begin to enjoy the fruits
of full, first-class citizenship? Would the white majority *ever* be willing to revise or abandon its preconceptions about inherent Negro inferiority?

As even the reform spirit generated in the Progressive Era passed them by in the main, and as, in the
1920s, the white Anglo-Saxon Protestant majority of
the nation seemed intent on reducing still more cat-
egories of "inferior" immigrant Americans to a status
of second-class citizenship, the Negroes' hopes for recognition under the Washington formula sank to a low
point, indeed. While Ku Klux Klansmen again roamed
the country and gained influence even in the highest
realms of national politics, the evidence seemed overwhelming that most white Americans considered the
Negro question settled. It had been settled in the same
way that the "Yellow Peril" presented by Oriental im-

migrants had been settled. Only in the case of the Negro that settlement assumed even harsher forms, and
blighted the lives of an even larger number of human
beings.

In the meantime, the North had come to know the
Negro and the Negro problem at closer range than
ever before. World War I created an enormous demand for workers in defense plants, most of which
were located in Northern cities. Like millions of immigrants from abroad searching for economic improvement before them, Southern Negroes uprooted themselves and trekked to New York, Philadelphia, Chicago, Detroit, and lesser industrial centers. Between
1910 and 1920 an estimated 350,000 took part in this
vast internal migration, and many others followed in
the years thereafter.

Again like the successive waves of foreign immigrants who had preceded them, however, the city-
bound Northern Negroes found themselves occupying
the bottom rung of society's ladder. They held the
worst jobs and lived in the worst housing in the worst
neighborhoods of the cities. They knew little about
coping with urban life; fell prey to the same diseases
and vices of the slum tenements that had ravaged
their previous occupants; found family ties still further
weakened; and developed an element of juvenile and
adult delinquents willing to try "the easy way out."

To the usual economic handicaps and cultural
discriminations suffered by the immigrant newcomers,
however, there was added in the Negroes' case the element of racial prejudice and discrimination from
which Northern whites, it soon turned out, were not

immune. His color made it easy to exclude even the most aspiring and skilled Negro from better jobs and housing, from the labor unions, from colleges, from public facilities, and from social contacts with his white neighbors.

Even more than the Irish, the Italians, and other European immigrant groups, therefore, the Northern Negroes found themselves reliant on social institutions and organizations of their own devising. As Negro communities appeared in cities throughout the North after the First World War, so too did colored fraternal societies, churches, newspapers and magazines, places of entertainment and amusement, and purveyors of professional services. Harlem and the "Little Harlems" were the centers of these activities, and in some respects they resembled the "Irish shanty-towns" and "Little Italys" that occupied other parts of the city. But there was this important difference: namely, the likelihood that the Negro individual's entire life—and that of his children and grandchildren—would be lived out within the constricting confines of the depressing environment he had known from the beginning. Not destined for the Negroes was the upward social mobility that the Irish and the Italians and the others knew. For, like Chinatown and Little Tokyo, Little Harlem was a ghetto that offered little hope of group recognition or advancement for its inhabitants.

Of course, as individuals, a few Negroes from both the urban slum ghettoes of the North and the rural caste-bound system of the South were able to "escape" to some measure of personal success and recognition during the last quarter of the nineteenth century and the first quarter of our own. As usual, sports provided one outlet. In prize fighting, Jack Johnson and other Negro boxers challenged the supremacy that Irishmen had long exercised in the ring. Several Negroes competed in the Olympics and won laurels for exceptional prowess in track and field events. Paul Robeson ranked on All-American football teams in 1917 while he was a student at Rutgers, and then went on to win critical acclaim in the 1920s as a splendid bass-baritone concert performer. Distinctive Negro musical forms (especially Dixieland jazz and the blues) and Negro musicians had their devotees among both races, and during the 1920s Cab Calloway and other bandleaders became quite popular.

By heroic efforts some Negroes also acquired first-rate professional educations, and then went on to distinguish themselves in the intellectual and scientific worlds. Carter Woodson and W. E. B. DuBois were two Harvard-trained Negro historians. George Washington Carver, the famed Tuskegee Institute chemist, developed hundreds of useful products and synthetics from peanuts, cotton stalks, and other resources indigenous to the South.

But Negroes who were able to rise above the oppressive handicaps imposed on them by poverty, bigotry, and discriminatory legislation during the early part of this century were all the more exceptional because of their small number. Nor were even the most prominent among them permitted to forget for long the badges of "inferiority" that less fortunate members of their race were compelled to wear daily. Negro athletes, for example, were generally barred from playing professional baseball, football, and other team sports. Even a Cab Calloway or a George Washington Carver encountered the taboos of social discrimination and segregation frequently enough—taboos that were enforced by law as they traveled in the South, more often by "social custom" as they traveled in the North.

Yet the northward migration of significant numbers of Negroes after 1915 did prove to be a blessing—even though for a time it remained in disguise—for this long-suffering minority group. Life in the industrial centers of the North was difficult enough for Negroes but, generally speaking, it did afford them more economic opportunity than was available in the South. Moreover, in most cases the patterns of social discrimination and segregation that existed above the Mason-Dixon Line rested upon custom and habit only; usually they were not required or enforced by law and were therefore less rigid than in the South. Finally, despite whatever other indignities might be heaped on them in the North, Negroes there were able to cast ballots on election day, unimpeded by the kinds of barriers that the Southern states had erected. That advantage provided the Northern Negro with a weapon his Southern brother did not possess. It turned out to be a very important one.

Enjoying these fragmentary advantages and these minimal tastes of a larger freedom, the Negroes of the North took the lead in espousing a more immediate demand for rights that Booker T. Washington had been willing to postpone to the indefinite future. The organizational spearhead for this more militant strategy was provided first by the National Association for the

Advancement of Colored People. A biracial movement
initiated in 1909, the NAACP's Negro leadership has
numbered such able figures as W. E. B. DuBois, the
poet James Weldon Johnson, Walter White, and its
current director, Roy Wilkins. In more recent years, of
course, many other Negro and biracial organizations
have joined in the ambitious campaign that the
NAACP began.

Convinced that the law had been the major instrument of Negro oppression in the past, the NAACP set
out to make the law serve the cause of Negro relief
and progress in the future. It therefore launched many
test cases against state and municipal "Jim Crow"
statutes. Its first major national campaign, begun in
the 1920s, was waged on behalf of securing a federal
law against lynching—a barbarous practice that had
cost hundreds of Negroes (and many whites) their
lives without the benefit of a court trial. As we have
seen, the decade of the 1920s was an inauspicious period for the cause of minority rights, and by its close the
NAACP and its allies had little to show for their efforts.

The 1930s brought greater economic distress than
ever before for Negroes and for the poor of America in
general (colored men, generally "the last to be hired"
in good times, often found themselves "the first to be
fired" when business took a turn for the worse). But at
the same time the Great Depression, by highlighting
the abuses present in the American system and com-
pelling attention to the plight of the nation's underpriv-
ileged elements, produced another upsurge of reform
sentiment. This time the reformers—now called New
Dealers—did not overlook the Negro entirely.

In part the liberals' new concern with the colored population was due to the development of the Northern Negroes' own voting potential to a point of considerable strength. By this time a few Negro congressmen —the first since Reconstruction days fifty years earlier —were being elected from predominantly colored districts in Northern cities. And the dramatic shift of the Negro vote, from its traditional Republican allegiance to the side of Franklin D. Roosevelt, also impressed sensitive politicians with the potency of this minority-group element. By the late 1930s, for example, a majority in both houses of Congress was ready to support the anti-lynching bill. Nevertheless, Southern resort to filibuster tactics in the Senate still prevented its enactment, and President Roosevelt, fearing the loss of Southern Democratic support for what he deemed more essential matters, failed to meet the civil-rights issue head on. When the decade ended Negro Americans had reason to believe that they had helped put a friend and sympathizer in the White House; but still they had achieved no legislation, and little in the way of firm executive action, in their behalf.

The Second World War proved to be the major turning point in the modern struggle of America's oldest minority group to win recognition—just as it was a turning point in many other aspects of American and world history. For one thing, the war against the Axis stimulated a vital change in the attitude of white Americans toward ideas of racial superiority and inferiority—as we shall see in the next chapter. Equally important was the war's effects on the American Negroes' own psychology. Thousands of Negroes, from both the North and the South, served in the armed forces. Though they were still discriminated against in the Army and Navy, Negroes nonetheless experienced unprecedented opportunities to travel both in their own country and abroad, to savor a larger degree of independence and authority, to develop self-confidence, and in many other ways to broaden their horizons and their ambitions. Liberated for a while from the Northern ghetto and the rural Southern slum, Negroes resolved that their postwar life must be a better one. Having defended democracy abroad, they were determined more than ever before to defend and extend it in their own land.

On the home front, meanwhile, the demand for all-out production of war materiel had opened up opportunities for economic advancement never before available to Negroes. The need for maximum use of the nation's productive manpower had brought about the first modern instance of the national government's intervention on behalf of Negro rights. In June of 1941, facing the threat of a massive Negro protest "March on Washington," President Roosevelt issued an executive order creating a temporary, wartime Fair Employment Practices Commission to eliminate discrimination in plants and unions doing defense work. During the war years Negro spokesmen and their liberal white allies sought to enact legislation to make the FEPC permanent, to outlaw the poll tax, and in other respects to bring the law into play to redress the Negoes' grievances and to assure him a greater share of the Four Freedoms that had been proclaimed as America's postwar objectives for the world.

It was not surprising, therefore, that the postwar years witnessed the launching of a civil-rights crusade that was previously unmatched in its range, intensity, and results. Negro and biracial organizations devoted to promoting racial justice grew and multiplied. Fortunately for their cause, President Harry S. Truman proved willing to become the first modern chief executive to seek full entry of the federal government into the civil-rights field. In 1947 Truman created an advisory Committee on Civil Rights, and in a message to Congress the following year he endorsed many of the committee's recommendations for federal legislation. At the Democratic national convention in 1948 Southern delegates walked out and formed the Dixiecrat Party in protest against the Administration's liberal program. But the Democrats renominated—and re-elected—Truman on a platform containing the strongest civil-rights plank of modern times.

Although several Northern states enacted state FEPC and anti-discrimination laws between 1945 and 1952, President Truman was unable to save the federal FEPC or to secure any other civil-rights legislation from Congress as a result of Southern filibustering tactics. Nevertheless, by executive order Truman initiated the desegregation of the armed forces and banned discrimination in federal employment and work done under government contract.

President Eisenhower, who took office in 1953, continued and expanded Truman's efforts in the area of executive action. But it was the Eisenhower-appointed Chief Justice of the United States, Earl Warren, who in 1954 wrote the Supreme Court's unanimous opinion in a case that established a major landmark in the civil-rights movement. In *Brown* v. *Board of Education of Topeka, Kansas* the Court struck down the "separate but equal" doctrine of *Plessy* v. *Ferguson.* "Separate educational facilities are inherently unequal," the Court decreed, and it found state laws requiring segregated schools to be in violation of the Fourteenth Amendment. Since 1954 the Supreme Court has applied its new interpretation to many other aspects of human activity and contact.

Implementation of the Court's decisions has not been an easy matter, of course. Nevertheless, through litigation, demonstration, economic boycott, and voting-registration drives, civil-rights advocates have made large dents in the "Jim Crow" edifice even in the most recalcitrant Southern states. Moreover, since 1957 their efforts have received increasing support by the direct intervention of the federal government. In that year Congress passed its first civil-rights act since 1875, authorizing the Attorney General to seek court injunctions against obstruction or deprivation of voting rights. Additional voting-rights acts passed in 1960 and 1965 involved the federal government even more effectively in guaranteeing Negroes their right to use the most powerful instrument that a minority group in our country can wield—the ballot.

During the first half of the 1960s, under the prodding of Presidents John F. Kennedy and Lyndon B. Johnson, Congress moved into civil-rights areas far beyond the field of voting rights. In 1963 Kennedy endorsed a civil-rights "package" measure that would authorize the federal government to exercise leadership and to engage actively in the process of desegregating schools and public accommodations and facilities (such as hotels, motels, restaurants, and public parks and playgrounds). The government might also cut off federal funds to grants-in-aid programs in areas which did not spread the benefits equally between Negroes and whites. Finally, the bill would establish a federal Equal Employment Opportunity Commission with authority to stop discrimination in most businesses and unions.

President Kennedy did not live to see his recommendations become effective. But in his first address to Congress following Kennedy's tragic assassination, President Lyndon B. Johnson called for "the earliest possible passage of the civil rights bill" as a fitting memorial to his slain predecessor. In June, after three months of Southern obstruction, the Senate took the unprecedented step of voting to impose cloture on a civil-rights filibuster. On July 2 Johnson signed the epochal Civil Rights Act of 1964 into law.

By the mid-sixties, then, Negro Americans could feel that the law—so long an instrument of their oppression—had been turned decisively at last into a vehicle for their advancement. Moreover, in the momentous era since the Second World War intolerance and discrimination had toppled in many areas of American life other than that of the law. Negro athletes, led by long-time heavyweight champion Joe Louis and track star Jesse Owens, had become more prominent and popular than ever. In 1947 Jackie Robinson became the first Negro to break the color barrier in professional baseball, and players such as Roy

Campanella, Don Newcombe, Hank Aaron, and Willie Mays soon became the heroes of colored and white fans alike. Negro musicians and performers such as Duke Ellington, Count Basie, Louis Armstrong, Pearl Bailey, Lena Horne, Nat "King" Cole, and Harry Belafontè won the hearts of nationwide audiences, and increasingly the nation's popular music showed the influence of the Negro idiom. Another color line fell when the brilliant contralto Marian Anderson—who had been denied the use of Constitution Hall in Washington for a concert in the early 1940s—made her debut with the Metropolitan Opera in 1955. By the mid-1960s Negro vocalists such as Metropolitan Opera soprano Leontyne Price and actors such as Sidney Poitier and Bill Cosby could aspire to the highest accolades that their arts and professions accorded.

In the postwar period, too, many businesses and labor unions voluntarily abandoned discriminatory practices against Negro job-seekers. The nation's private colleges and universities lowered and abolished racial bars where they had existed before; even college fraternities began to give way to the new tide of racial "fraternization." Meanwhile, thousands of Negro veterans utilized the GI Bill of Rights to gain training in every field of education. One result has been a growing number of Negro doctors, lawyers, professional men, and public servants. Few Americans in public life could claim more international respect than Dr. Ralph J. Bunche, a former Harvard University political science professor who, as Under Secretary of the United Nations, won the Nobel Peace Prize in 1950. Under President Johnson, Thurgood Marshall, who

had headed the NAACP's legal department, became
the first Negro to occupy a seat on the United States
Supreme Court. In 1965 Dr. Robert C. Weaver became the first Secretary of the newly established Department of Housing and Urban Development, as well
as the first Negro to occupy a place in the cabinet.

The increasing contributions that Negro Americans
have been enabled to make to human welfare in the
recent period of greater opportunity have proven,
once and for all, the absurdity of the charges of inherent racial inferiority lodged against them in earlier
times. Yet old prejudices against ethnic groups, especially those reinforced by distinctions of color, die
slowly. It appears certain, therefore, that agitation
over the issue of Negro civil rights will continue in the
near future and that additional legislation will be necessary to guarantee enjoyment of those rights. This
continuing need to bring the law to the assistance of
the Negroes' quest for recognition and equal opportunity frequently confuses and disturbs white Americans, especially the members of immigrant ethnic
groups whose own minority status is receding into the
past. "Why do Negroes need special laws?" the descendants of Irish or Italian immigrants sometimes
ask. "Why don't they just lift themselves up by their
own boot straps, the way my people did?"

Those who ask the questions overlook the point concerning Negro Americans made at the beginning of
this chapter: that no other among our many ethnic
groups has ever been so completely denied, *by law*,
the opportunities for social mobility and individual

advancement that America offers its inhabitants. When the time came that the "native" Yankee was ready to forget his prejudices and to sit down with his Catholic Irish neighbor "to play . . . at dominoes or checkers," a mere private act of the will was all that was necessary. In the case of the white man and the Negro, on the other hand, a resort to public *law* might first be necessary, in order to make their private action legal.

In other words when public law and not mere private ignorance has been used to encrust ethnic prejudice, then the law must be used, as a supplement to education, to end ethnic injustice. And so long as Negroes rest their efforts to correct injustice on the law and on peaceful methods, white Americans need have no fear for the nation's health, safety, and welfare.

It is understandable, on the other hand, that after three and a half centuries of oppression Negroes should sometimes display impatience with the relatively slow process of legal redress of their grievances. Even as the pace of that process has quickened in recent years, the tendency to resort to violence has increased among the more radical elements of the Negro rights movement. But given the framework of American society and the history of ethnic-group relations in this country, the 10 per cent of our population who are Negroes would do well to heed the words of one of their most respected and effective leaders, Nobel Prize winner Martin Luther King. "In the process of gaining our rightful place," Dr. King counseled on the occasion of 1963's peacefully impressive March on Washington in support of civil-rights legislation, "we must not be guilty of wrongful deeds." The discredit that came to the Molly Maguires a century ago, when members of another exploited minority group turned to terrorist tactics that only damaged their cause, well proves the wisdom of those words.

For it is a fact of life, which American minorities of every sort must live with, that in the United States democracy is the rule—no matter how unjust its rule may be at times. Consequently, the status of a minority is established in the last analysis by the majority, and no minority—no matter how just its cause or how strenuous its efforts in its own behalf—can move far or effectively without gaining sympathetic allies among the majority elements. The impressive strides made by Negro Americans since the 1930s owe much to the new militancy generated among Negroes themselves. But they owe something, too, to changes that have taken place in the thinking of the white majority since the 1920s, when even serious candidates for the Presidency felt compelled to kow-tow to the Ku Klux Klan. In contrast to the narrow and divisive sort of nationalism which prevailed in that decade, marking the modern nadir of hope for Negroes and other "undesirable" ethnic minorities, stand now the sentiments of President Kennedy as he explained to his countrymen the need for sweeping civil-rights legislation in 1963:

> This is one country. It has become one country because all of us and all the people who came here had an equal chance to develop their talents. We cannot say to ten per cent of the population

that they can't have that right; that their children
can't have the chance to develop whatever talents
they have; that the only way that they are going
to get their rights is to go into the streets and
demonstrate. I think we owe them and we owe
ourselves a better country than that.

In this statement the President measured not only
the large distance that Americans have yet to go in according recognition and equal opportunity to their
oldest and largest minority group. He measured also
the tremendous distance they had come in the period
of his own adulthood in developing a broader, more
liberal, and "pluralistic" definition of Americanism
that would prove capable, hopefully, of bearing the
strains of the future.

VII. CONCLUSION: BUILDING A NATION

THE NATIVIST AND RACIST "100 per cent American" movement of the 1920s produced various reactions among the supposedly undesirable ethnic minority groups who were its victims. Told that they failed to measure up to the standards of "real Americanism" as defined by the dominant older inhabitants of the land, some members of the Negro and New Immigrant groups identified themselves more closely than ever with "homelands" or causes which seemed more appreciative of them. Thus, some Italian-Americans joined the Fascist League of North America, which was supported by the Italian dictator Benito Mussolini. Perhaps a few Japanese-Americans became more favorable to the expansionist ambitions of the militaristic elements in the Japanese government in Tokyo. Among Negroes there developed briefly a "Back to Africa" movement, led by one Marcus Garvey, which attempted to substitute black nationalism and African culture in place of the Negroes' American ties. Other disillusioned people enlisted in the Communist Party, which made great efforts to recruit supporters among the minorities rejected by the native Americans. Certainly these kinds of reverse nationalism, and the divisive tendencies they created in the United States, were just the opposite of what the American nativist groups had hoped to achieve.

But the results attained by Fascists, Communists, and all others who tried to bend to their own purposes the frustrations of America's minority groups must have been disappointing. For despite the humiliation heaped upon them by the dominant white Anglo-Saxon Protestant majority, most Newer Americans refused to transfer their loyalty to another nation or cause. Instead, they rejected the claim of the nativists and racists that all true citizens must conform to one ethnic and cultural pattern and be able to trace their ancestry back to only one part of Europe. Spokesmen for the minority groups, and for those old-stock people who opposed nativism, argued rather for acceptance of a more tolerant pluralistic definition of Americanism.

Conceding that assimilation by the minorities to the dominant natives' ways of life, in many aspects, was desirable and inevitable, the "cultural pluralists" nonetheless denied that *total* cultural, religious, and racial uniformity was essential to the nation's welfare. If provided with good environments and equal opportunity, they contended, individuals from among all of America's different ethnic, religious, and racial groups possessed the potential for contributing to the country's material and cultural advancement. Complete melting away of ethnic differences was not only impossible but undesirable. For total conformity would deprive the nation of one of the sources of vitality and enrichment which it had enjoyed from its birth.

The cultural pluralists were correct, then—like the nativists—in recognizing that the melting-pot theory has failed to work, at least with total thoroughness. But in place of the substitute for the melting pot which the nativists proposed—conformity to the dominant group's narrow conception of Americanism—the pluralists argued for tolerance of ethnic and cultural variety. If a man worked hard, and thus contributed to his own and the country's advancement; if he obeyed the laws and responded to the call to duty when the nation was endangered, then it made little difference that his color, his national origins, his religion, or his customs and traditions varied from those of the majority. He had a right to capitalize on the opportunities which this country offered, to the limit of his own talents and abilities. The national welfare, in turn, would benefit not only economically from his labors but also culturally from the richness and variety which he and the members of his group might be able to contribute out of their own distinctive culture.

Gradually, and with time, the arguments of the cultural pluralists have made headway against the doctrines of narrow "100 per cent Americanism." In part this transformation is due to rather negative factors. For after the adoption of the immigration restriction laws of the 1920s, "foreigners" and "foreign" ways did become less prominent on the American scene. Second and third generations of immigrant children affected by the leveling influence of an American education, did "assimilate" more than their parents had. At the same time, improvements in the means of transportation and communication—especially the movies, radio, and television—have tended to make American society and culture more homogeneous and uniform. In short, ethnic, religious, and cultural differences within the American population became less sharp and less visible as time passed. And the smaller the differences that separate various groups are, the easier it is for them to be tolerant of one another.

But in addition, more positive developments have also contributed to the rise of pluralistic Americanism and the decline of narrow nationalism and racism. For one thing, in recent years the researches of anthropologists and sociologists such as Alfred Kroeber and Earnest Hooten have exploded the myths, once masked as "science," that supported racist doctrines earlier. Experts today no longer believe in the ideas of superior and inferior racial inheritance that underlay, for example, the report of the Dillingham Commission in 1911. In fact, in 1939 the American Anthropological Association adopted a resolution stating that "Anthropology provides no scientific basis for discrimination against any people on the ground of racial inferiority, religious affiliation, or linguistic heritage." Thus present-day science confirms that which the practical contributions to human betterment made by individuals from all of our minority groups establishes in a common-sense way.

Moreover, from the 1920s onward minority groups have become increasingly important in terms of the number of votes and the political power they wield, particularly in the large and politically crucial industrial, urban states. Al Smith, their first political champion in national politics, demonstrated their growing strength in 1928 by carrying for the Democrats a number of big cities, as well as the states of Massachusetts and Rhode Island, which had normally voted Republican before. Thereafter politicians were compelled to become more considerate of the minority groups' votes, and therefore more responsive to their demands for recognition as first-class citizens.

At the same time, the idealism and reform spirit generated by the Great Depression and the New Deal of the 1930s created a climate of opinion more favorable to fulfillment of both the economic and psychological needs of America's common men—among whom our various minority groups numbered. The New Deal's leader, President Franklin D. Roosevelt, who qualified as a native descended from colonial settlers, nonetheless sided with the minorities' point of view both out of recognition of their growing political power and because of his own humanitarian sympathy for the oppressed. He lent the power of his voice and his prestige to the cause of cultural pluralism when, in 1937, for example, he urged the members of the Daughters of the American Revolution to "Remember, remember always, that all of us, and you and I especially, are descended from immigrants. . . ."

Then came the Second World War in which Americans—including large contingents from all of the nation's minority groups—successfully took up arms against a coalition of dictators who represented the greatest threat ever posed against this country's ideals of democracy, freedom, and respect for the dignity of the individual. Wartime experience not only quickened the minority-group GI's demand for greater respect and more decent treatment when he returned home. Travel, common danger, fraternization, and broadened cultural contact also affected the outlook of "native" servicemen. Association with "buddies" who belonged to hitherto unfamiliar religions, nationalities, and races frequently shook old preconceptions. Biases and prejudices were re-examined, and greater tolerance of ethnic diversity was the over-all result. Moreover, the war was fought against enemies—and Adolph Hitler's Nazis in particular—who espoused doctrines of racial superiority of their own and who applied them in the most ruthless fashion imaginable. Understandably, then, the appeal of racist thinking declined in the United States as a result of our crusade to guarantee the Four Freedoms to all the peoples of the world.

Next there followed the Cold War and a worldwide contest with communism. In this contest the United States has been called upon, as never before, to demonstrate the superiority of her way of life as the best means of affording opportunity for advancement to even the humblest members of the human race. Our ideals of liberty and freedom can no longer be merely *talked* about; they must be rigorously applied and lived up to. For an important audience across the entire world is sitting in judgment between the worth of the ways of freedom and the ways of communism. Since a large part of that audience consists of colored peoples—who have in the past been treated as minorities by the major Western powers—our treatment of our own minorities becomes crucial in determining the outcome of the contest. Cultural pluralism and tolerance of diversity are the attitudes we must now adopt toward the peoples of the world; surely they must be our attitudes toward the ethnic elements that go into the making of our own population here at home.

Propelled by this complex of developments, then, Americans have gradually substituted the broader and more tolerant doctrines of cultural pluralism—or cultural liberalism—in place of the narrow, restrictive, and conservative definition of 100 per cent Americanism that held sway in the 1920s. It is good that such is the direction in which our national attitudes are moving, for America still is, and there are strong indications that she will always be, a country of ethnic diversity in which minorities remain prominent. Our present-day internal minorities—especially Chinese- and Japanese-Americans, Puerto Ricans, Negroes, Mexican-Americans, and American Indians, among others—still labor under severe handicaps imposed by prejudice and discrimination. It will be some time yet before we truly bring into being for all of our present citizens "a cultural democracy, based on mutual understanding and appreciation."

Moreover, the piecemeal relaxation of immigration restrictions that took place during and after the Second World War augmented once again the number of "newcomers" from abroad among us. True enough, as late as 1952 Congress preserved in the McCarran-Walter Immigration Act the inequitable quota system adopted in the 1920s—a system that, as President Truman declared in his unsuccessful veto message, erected unjustifiable barriers against Catholics, Jews, and southern and eastern Europeans. But the McCarran-

Walter Act itself did grant small quotas to Asian countries from which immigration had been banned altogether previously. In the meantime, Congress enacted
separate legislation during the late 1940s and the 1950s
admitting thousands of displaced persons, refugees
from communist oppression, and foreign-born wives
of American servicemen serving overseas.

Then in the mid-1960s, under President Johnson's
vigorous prodding and after every President since
Truman had urged it, Congress finally abandoned altogether the nativist-inspired immigration quota system of the 1920s. The Immigration Act of 1965 provides that henceforth there shall be an annual ceiling
of 170,000 immigrants from all nations outside the
Western Hemisphere, with a limit of 20,000 from any
single country (exempting parents, spouses, and children of American citizens). Preference will be given
to refugees, persons with close relatives in the United
States, and workers possessing skills needed in the nation's economy. But gone under the new system are
the antiquated distinctions between allegedly superior
and inferior races or nationalities, and it fully measures up to President Johnson's admonition that our
immigration laws "ask not where a person comes from,
but what are his personal qualities." "No move," the
President added, "could more effectively reaffirm our
fundamental belief that a man is to be judged—and
judged exclusively—on his worth as a human being."

As the country's new—or restored—policy of non-
discriminatory immigration takes effect, it can be expected that the number of "more different" immigrants
coming from southern and eastern Europe, Asia, and

other areas formerly deemed undesirable will swell. This result will enlarge those more recently arrived elements of our population who today remain closest to minority status, and may perhaps introduce still newer ingredients into the human mixture that makes up the American nation.

Such prospects indicate that the basic pattern of ethnic diversity, conflict, and mutual adjustment that has marked American history will continue in the future. But in retrospect it should be evident that this pattern has made a vital contribution—despite the national problems and individual heartbreak that accompanied it—to America's economic and cultural vitality and to the continual rejuvenation of its dedication to the ideals of personal and political freedom. President John F. Kennedy described the process very well when he wrote that

> Each new group was met by the groups already in America, and adjustment was often difficult and painful. The early English settlers had to find ways to get along with the Indians; the Irish who followed were met by these "Yankees"; German immigrants faced both Yankees and Irish; and so it has gone down to the latest group of Hungarian refugees. Somehow, the difficult adjustments are made and people get down to the tasks of earning a living, raising a family, living with their new neighbors and, in the process, building a nation.

And "every ethnic minority," President Kennedy added, "in seeking its own freedom, helped strengthen the fabric of liberty in American life."

The process of building the American nation, economically and culturally, is far from completed. Nor can the fabric of liberty in American life ever be made too strong. For both purposes, America can well afford to act upon the principles which cultural pluralism dictates, both as to the nature of our immigration policy and the treatment of our internal "minority" groups.

Moreover, by installing the dictates of cultural liberalism as our guide in the future, Americans will only be returning to the ideals of the most revered of their Founding Fathers. In 1783 George Washington declared:

> The bosom of America is open to receive not only the opulent and respectable stranger, but the oppressed and persecuted of all nations and religions; whom we shall welcome to a participation in all our rights and privileges, if by decency and propriety of conduct they appear to merit the enjoyment.

The history of America's ethnic minority groups, which is the history of America's success, points the way.

APPENDICES

1607 English "immigrants" establish first permanent British colony at Jamestown, Virginia

1619 First Negroes are put ashore at Jamestown

1623 Settlement of New Netherland (New York) by Dutch West India Company

1634 Lord Baltimore founds Maryland as a refuge for English Catholics

1649 Maryland Toleration Act extends religious freedom to all groups professing trinitarian Christianity

1664 Maryland legislature enacts first formal "Slave Code"

1681 William Penn founds Pennsylvania as a refuge for Quakers

1685 Revocation of Edict of Nantes by King Louis XIV causes French Huguenots to migrate to America, especially to South Carolina

1700–1776 Immigrant Germans, Scots, and Scotch-Irish become an increasingly important part of the colonial population

1740 Parliament enacts Naturalization Act conferring

British citizenship on alien immigrants in American colonies

1776   Declaration of Independence: "That all men are created equal. . . ."

1776–1800   Slavery outlawed in Northern states

1798   Naturalization, Alien and Sedition Acts passed by Federalists in attempt to limit growing political importance of immigrants supporting Jeffersonian Republicans

1808   Further importation of Negro slaves is prohibited

1840s Irish potato famine causes many to migrate to America. Large-scale immigration from Great Britain, Germany, and the Scandinavian countries also under way

1850s Nativist, anti-immigrant Know-Nothing Party attains political strength in several states

1864   Importation of contract labor made legal by Congress

1865   Thirteenth Amendment abolishes slavery

1868   Fourteenth Amendment declares all persons born or naturalized in the United States to be citizens; forbids states to abridge rights of citizens

1870   Fifteenth Amendment forbids states to deny citizens the right to vote on account of race or color

1880s Large-scale immigration under way from countries of southern and eastern Europe

1882   First federal immigration law bars lunatics, idiots, convicts and those likely to become public charges

1882   Chinese Exclusion Act passed by Congress

1885   Congress prohibits importation of contract labor

1890s Rise of nativist, anti-Catholic American Protective Association

1891   Congress adds health qualifications to immigration restrictions

1894   Immigration Restriction League founded

1896   Supreme Court establishes "separate but equal" doctrine regarding segregation in *Plessy* v. *Ferguson* case

1903   Immigration law bars anarchists and persons believing in forcible overthrow of government

1908   "Gentlemen's Agreement" with Japan

1909   National Association for the Advancement of Colored People founded

1911   Dillingham Commission established by Congress reports on immigration

1917   Congress establishes literacy test for immigrants

1920s Resurgence of nativist, anti-Negro Ku Klux Klan

1921   Emergency immigration restriction law begins quota system, heavily weighted in favor of countries of northern and western Europe

1924   National Origins Act establishes discriminatory immigration quota system as permanent policy; prohibits immigration from Asian countries altogether

1928   Defeat of Al Smith in presidential election initiates "unwritten" rule that "no Catholic can be President"

1941   Executive order creates temporary Fair Employment Practices Commission

1942   Japanese-Americans evacuated from Pacific Coast to inland detention camps

1943   Chinese Exclusion Act repealed; China given token quota

1945   Large-scale immigration from Puerto Rico begins

1946   War Brides Act provides for admission of foreign-born wives of American servicemen

1948   President Truman urges Congress to enact civil-rights legislation; executive orders begin desegregation of armed forces and end discrimination in federal employment

1948   Displaced Persons Act provides for admission of war refugees

1952   Congress passes McCarran-Walter Immigration Act over President Truman's veto. Continues discriminatory immigration quota system, but grants token quotas to Asian countries

1953   Refugee Relief Act provides for admission of additional refugees

1954   Supreme Court upsets the "separate but equal" doctrine in *Brown* v. *Board of Education of Topeka, Kansas;* begins new era of constitutional interpretation regarding civil-rights cases

1957   Special legislation admits refugees following anti-Communist uprisings in Hungary

1957   Congress passes Voting Rights Act; first civil-rights legislation since 1875

1960   Congress passes additional voting-rights legislation

1960   John F. Kennedy becomes first Catholic to be elected President

1962   Executive order forbids racial discrimination in
       federally assisted housing
1964   Twenty-fourth Amendment outlaws poll tax in
       elections for federal offices
1964   Congress passes sweeping Civil Rights Act of
       1964
1965   Congress enacts additional voting-rights legis-
       lation
1965   Immigration Act ends discriminatory quota
       system

My Fellow Americans: I am about to sign into law the Civil Rights Act of 1964. I want to take this occasion to talk to you about what that law means to every American.

188 years ago this week a small band of valiant men began a long struggle for freedom. They pledged their lives, their fortunes, and their sacred honor not only to found a nation, but to forge an ideal of freedom—not only for political independence, but for personal liberty—not only to eliminate foreign rule, but to establish the rule of justice in the affairs of men.

That struggle was a turning point in our history. Today in far corners of distant continents, the ideals of those American patriots still shape the struggles of men who hunger for freedom.

This is a proud triumph. Yet those who founded our country knew that freedom would be secure only if each generation fought to renew and enlarge its meaning. From the Minutemen at Concord to the soldiers in Viet Nam, each generation has been equal to that trust.

Americans of every race and color have died in

battle to protect our freedom. Americans of every race and color have worked to build a nation of widening opportunities. Now our generation of Americans has been called on to continue the unending search for justice within our own borders.

We believe that all men are created equal. Yet many are denied equal treatment. We believe that all men have certain unalienable rights. Yet many Americans do not enjoy those rights. We believe that all men are entitled to the blessings of liberty. Yet millions are being deprived of those blessings—not because of their own failures, but because of the color of their skin.

The reasons are deeply imbedded in history and tradition and the nature of man. We can understand—without rancor or hatred—how this all happened.

But it cannot continue. Our Constitution, the foundation of our Republic, forbids it. The principles of our freedom forbid it. Morality forbids it. And the law I will sign tonight forbids it.

That law is the product of months of the most careful debate and discussion. It was proposed more than one year ago by our late and beloved President John F. Kennedy. It received the bipartisan support of more than two-thirds of the Members of both the House and Senate. An overwhelming majority of Republicans as well as Democrats voted for it.

It has received the thoughtful support of tens of thousands of civic and religious leaders in all parts of this Nation. And it is supported by the great majority of the American people.

The purpose of the law is simple. It does not restrict the freedom of any American so long as he respects the rights of others. It does not give special treatment to any citizen.

It does say that those who are equal before God shall now also be equal in the polling booths, in the classrooms, in the factories, and in hotels, restaurants, movie theaters, and other places that provide service to the public. . . .

We must not approach the observance and enforcement of this law in a vengeful spirit. Its purpose is not to punish. Its purpose is not to divide, but to end divisions—divisions which have all lasted too long. Its purpose is national, not regional. Its purpose is to promote a more abiding commitment to freedom, a more constant pursuit of justice, and a deeper respect for human dignity.

We will achieve these goals because most Americans are law-abiding citizens who want to do what is right. That is why the Civil Rights Act relies first on voluntary compliance, then on the efforts of local communities and states to secure the rights of citizens. It provides for the national authority to step in only when others cannot or will not do the job.

This Civil Rights Act is a challenge to all of us to go to work in our communities and our states, in our homes and in our hearts, to eliminate the last vestiges of injustice in our beloved America.

So tonight I urge every public official, every religious leader, every business and professional man, every working man, every housewife—I urge every

American—to join in this effort to bring justice and hope to all our people—and to bring peace to our land.

My fellow citizens, we have come now to a time of testing. We must not fail.

Let us close the springs of racial poison. Let us pray for wise and understanding hearts. Let us lay aside irrelevant differences and make our Nation whole. Let us hasten that day when our unmeasured strength and our unbounded spirit will be free to do the great works ordained for this Nation by the just and wise God who is the Father of us all.

This bill that we sign today is not a revolutionary bill. It does not affect the lives of millions. It will not reshape the structure of our daily lives, or really add importantly to either our wealth or our power.

Yet it is still one of the most important acts of this Congress and of this Administration.

For it does repair a very deep and painful flaw in the fabric of American justice. It corrects a cruel and enduring wrong in the conduct of the American nation. . . .

This bill says simply that from this day forth those wishing to emigrate to America shall be admitted on the basis of their skills and their close relationship to those already here.

This is a simple test, and it is a fair test. Those who can contribute most to this country—to its growth, to its strength, to its spirit—will be the first that are admitted to this land.

The fairness of this standard is so self-evident that we may well wonder that it has not always been applied. Yet the fact is that for over four decades the immigration policy of the United States has been twisted and has been distorted by the harsh injustice of the National Origins Quota System.

Under that system the ability of new immigrants to come to America depended upon the country of their birth. Only three countries were allowed to supply seventy percent of all the immigrants.

Families were kept apart because a husband or a wife or a child had been born in the wrong place.

Men of needed skill and talent were denied entrance because they came from southern or eastern Europe or from one of the developing continents.

This system violated the basic principle of American democracy—the principle that values and rewards each man on the basis of his merit as a man.

It has been un-American in the highest sense because it has been untrue to the faith that brought thousands to these shores even before we were a country.

Today, with my signature, this system is abolished.

We can now believe that it will never again shadow the gate to the American nation with the twin barriers of prejudice and privilege.

Our beautiful America was built by a nation of strangers. From a hundred different places or more, they have poured forth into an empty land—joining and blending in one mighty and irresistible tide.

The land flourished because it was fed from so many sources—because it was nourished by so many cultures and traditions and peoples.

And from this experience, almost unique in the history of nations, has come America's attitude toward the rest of the world. We, because of what we are, feel safer and stronger in a world as varied as the people who make it up—a world where no country rules another and all countries can deal with the basic problems of human dignity and deal with those problems in their own way.

Now, under the monument which has welcomed so many to our shores, the American nation returns to the finest of its traditions today.

The days of unlimited immigration are past.

But those who do come will come because of what they are, and not because of the land from which they sprung.

When the earliest settlers poured into a wild continent there was no one to ask them where they came from. The only question was: Were they sturdy enough to make the journey, were they strong enough to clear the land, were they enduring enough to make a home for freedom, and were they brave enough to die for liberty if it became necessary to do so.

And so it has been through all the great and testing moments of American history. This year we see in Viet Nam men dying—men named Fernandez and Zajac and Zelinko and Mariano and McCormick.

Neither the enemy who killed them nor the people whose independence they have fought to save ever asked them where they or their parents came from. They were all Americans. It was for free men and for America that they gave their all, they gave their lives and selves.

By eliminating that same question as a test for

immigration the Congress proves ourselves worthy of those men and worthy of our own traditions as a nation. . . .

Over my shoulder here you can see Ellis Island, whose vacant corridors echo today the joyous sounds of long-ago voices.

And today we can all believe that the lamp of this grand old lady is brighter today—and the golden door that she guards gleams more brilliantly in the light of an increased liberty for the people from all the countries of the globe.

BENSON, ADOLPH B., and NABOTH HEDIN. *Americans from Sweden.* Philadelphia: J. B. Lippincott Company, 1950.

BERNARD, WILLIAM S., *et al.*, eds. *American Immigration Policy.* New York: Harper, 1950.

BLEGEN, THEODORE C. *Norwegian Migration to America, 1825–1860.* Northfield, Minn.: Norwegian-American History Association, 1940.

BOWERS, DAVID F., ed. *Foreign Influences in American Life.* Princeton, N.J.: Princeton University Press, 1944.

BROWN, FRANCIS J., and JOSEPH S. ROUČEK. *One America.* New York: Prentice-Hall, 1952.

DUCHARME, JACQUES. *The Shadows of the Trees: The Story of French-Canadians in New England.* New York: 1943.

FAUST, ALBERT B. *The German Element in the United States.* 2 vols. New York: Houghton, 1909.

FRANKLIN, JOHN HOPE. *From Slavery to Freedom: A History of American Negroes.* New York: Knopf, 1956.

GLAZER, NATHAN, and DANIEL MOYNIHAN. *Beyond*

the Melting Pot: the Negroes, Puerto Ricans, Jews, Italians, and Irish of New York City. Cambridge, Mass.: M. I. T. Press, 1963.

GOVORCHIN, G. G. *Americans from Yugoslavia.* Gainesville, Fla.: University of Florida Press, 1961.

HANDLIN, OSCAR. *Adventure in Freedom: Three Hundred Years of Jewish Life in America.* New York: McGraw-Hill, 1954.

————. *The American People in the Twentieth Century.* Cambridge, Mass.: Harvard University Press, 1959.

————. *Race and Nationality in American Life.* Boston: Little, Brown and Company, 1957.

————. *The Newcomers: Negroes and Puerto Ricans in a Changing Metropolis.* Garden City, New York: Doubleday & Company, 1962.

————. *The Uprooted: the Epic Story of the Great Migrations that Made the American People.* Boston: Little, Brown and Company, 1952.

HIGHAM, JOHN. *Strangers in the Land.* New Brunswick, N.J.: Rutgers University Press, 1955.

HITTI, PHILIP K. *The Syrians in America.* New York: George H. Doran, 1924.

HOGLUND, WILLIAM A. *Finnish Immigrants in America.* Madison, Wisc.: University of Wisconsin Press, 1960.

KENNEDY, JOHN F. *A Nation of Immigrants.* New York: Harper & Row, 1964.

KUNG, S. W. *Chinese in American Life.* Seattle: University of Washington Press, 1962.

LENGYEL, EMIL. *Americans from Hungary.* Philadelphia: J. B. Lippincott Company, 1948.

LUCAS, HENRY S. *Netherlanders in America.* Ann Arbor, Mich.: University of Michigan Press, 1955.

MCWILLIAMS, CAREY. *Brothers under the Skin.* rev. ed. Boston: Little, Brown and Company, 1964.

————. *North from Mexico.* New York: Monthly Review Press, 1961.

PADILLA, ELENA. *Up from Puerto Rico.* New York: Columbia University Press, 1958.

QUARLES, BENJAMIN. *The Negro in the Making of America.* New York: Collier Books, 1964.

Revolution in Civil Rights. Washington: Congressional Quarterly Service, 1966.

SALOUTOS, THEODORE. *The Greeks in the United States.* Cambridge, Mass.: Harvard University Press, 1963.

SCHERMERHORN, R. A. *These Our People: Minorities in American Culture.* Boston: D. C. Heath, 1949.

SHANNON, WILLIAM V. *The American Irish.* New York: Macmillan, 1963.

SOLOMON, BARBARA. *Ancestors and Immigrants.* Cambridge, Mass.: Harvard University Press, 1956.

SMITH, BRADFORD. *Americans from Japan.* Philadelphia: J. B. Lippincott Company, 1948.

WITTKE, CARL. *We Who Built America: the Saga of the Immigrant.* Cleveland: Western Reserve University Press, 1939.

WOODWARD, C. VANN. *The Strange Career of Jim Crow.* New York: Oxford University Press, 1966.

WYTRWAL, JOSEPH A. *America's Polish Heritage.* Detroit: Endurance Press, 1961.

INDEX